SCIMITAR

MICHAEL J. DOUST

FROM THE COCKPIT 2

INTRODUCTION

THE Supermarine Scimitar naval fighter and strike aircraft entered Royal Navy service in August 1957 with 700X Flight—the Intensive Flying Trials Unit (IFTU)—at RNAS Ford, near Arundel in Sussex. This unit was in existence for approximately nine months, carrying out the vital service evaluation and rectification work, and the first front-line unit, 803 Naval Air Squadron, was formed on 3 June 1958 at RNAS Lossiemouth, Scotland. Further squadrons—800, 804 and 807— were commissioned shortly thereafter, all based out of Lossiemouth. The last squadron to disband would be 803 NAS, on 1 October 1966: first in, last out!

The aircraft was, for a naval fighter at that time, big and very heavy. It was fitted with two powerful Rolls-Royce Avon turbojets and, unusually, these were not equipped with reheat (afterburner augmentation). Although the Scimitar could quite readily go supersonic in a dive, it could not achieve this while flying straight and level.

With the decommissioning of the Westland Wyvern strike squadrons and the withdrawal from service of that aircraft, the Scimitar took over the primary strike role in the Royal Navy, at the same time introducing to the Fleet Air Arm the capability of delivering an airborne nuclear weapon; within a decade, this role would be taken on in turn by the Blackburn Buccaneer strike bomber. The aircraft was quite capable of carrying a heavy conventional-ordnance load, including air-to-surface guided missiles, but, unlike its predecessor, it was never called upon to go war.

It was a powerful and wonderful fighter jet in the air, and thoroughly liked by all pilots who flew it. It was generally forgiving, and was quite capable of sustaining damage and still flying safely. With its huge undercarriage wheels, it could also operate from snow-packed runways if called upon to do so.

The Scimitar was not flown by any other naval air arm or air force, although Airwork Ltd, based at Hurn, did use the aircraft for various training tasks on behalf of the Royal Navy. It had been in front-line service for just over eight years when its strike role was taken over by the Buccaneer.

Right: Supermarine Scimitars of 800 Naval Air Squadron, 1961.

COURTESY PHILIP JARRETT

THREE

REQUIREMENT

THE Naval Staff Requirement from which the Scimitar evolved was designated N.113D; indeed, the aircraft was originally known simply as the Supermarine N.113. Its development followed a tortuous path, at least initially, involving the rather different Supermarine Types 508 and 529. These two aircraft had a straight wing and a 'butterfly' type tail, and apart from the latter feature, and the fact that two engines rather than one were installed, were not entirely dissimilar in appearance from the company's Attacker fighter that, in the early 1950s, was equipping front-line FAA squadrons. The 508 and 529 were followed by the radically different, swept-wing 525 and, after the loss of that aircraft, by the Type 544, which incorporated 'area ruling' in the fuselage and blown flaps to produce

Below: The Supermarine Type 525, the immediate forerunner of the Type 544, otherwise known as the N.113 and, ultimately, Scimitar.

FOUR

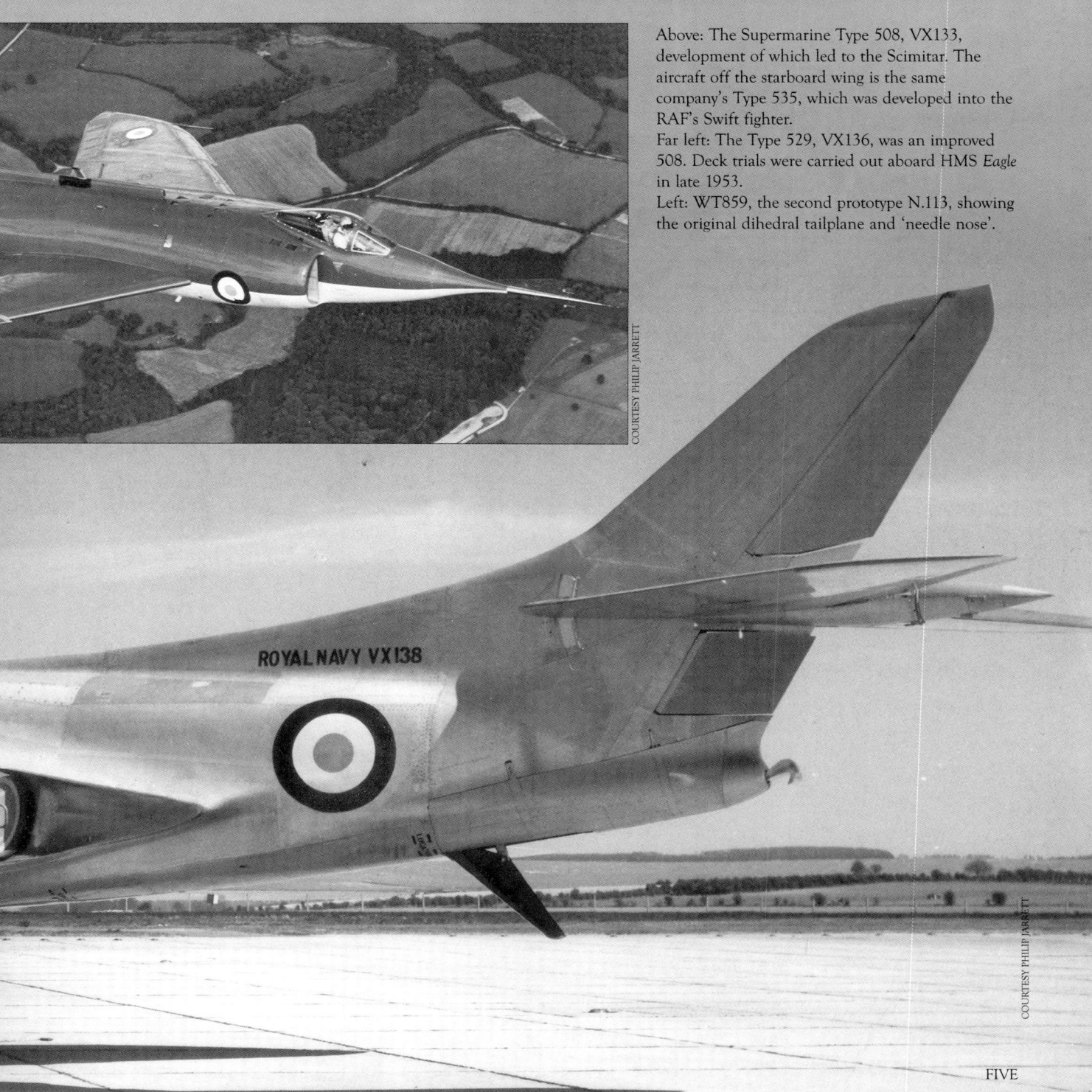

Above: The Supermarine Type 508, VX133, development of which led to the Scimitar. The aircraft off the starboard wing is the same company's Type 535, which was developed into the RAF's Swift fighter.
Far left: The Type 529, VX136, was an improved 508. Deck trials were carried out aboard HMS *Eagle* in late 1953.
Left: WT859, the second prototype N.113, showing the original dihedral tailplane and 'needle nose'.

SCIMITAR

> # SPECIFICATIONS
> ## SUPERMARINE SCIMITAR F. Mk 1
>
> Manufacturer: Supermarine Aircraft Company. Production line at South Marston, Swindon, Wiltshire.
> Design: Supermarine N.113.
> Chief Designer: Joseph Smith, FRAeS.
> Powerplant: Two Rolls-Royce Avon RA.24 or RA.26 each developing 10,000lb (4,535kg, 44.5kN) static thrust; later Avon 200 series, 11,250lb (5,100kg, 50.0kN).
> Dimensions: Length overall 55ft 3in (16.84m); wing span 37ft 2in (11.33m) spread, 20ft 6½in (6.26m) folded; height 17ft 4in (5.28m); wing area 484.9 sq ft (45.0m^2).
> Weights: 23,962lb (10,875kg) dry, 34,200lb (15,520kg) fully loaded.
> Armament: Four fixed 30mm Aden cannon (120rds/gun); maximum external load 8,000lb (3,630kg).
> Performance: Max. speed 640kts (735mph, 1,185kph, Mach 0.966) at sea level, 585kts (675mph, 1,090kph, Mach 0.992) at 30,000ft (9,150m); climb to 45,000 ft (13,700m), 6.65min; service ceiling 46,000ft (14,000m); normal range 1,230nm (1,420 miles, 2,290km) at 35,000ft (10,670m).

Below: XD212, the first production Supermarine Scimitar. A more tapered nose profile was quickly introduced on later production aircraft, in order to improve the view forward for the pilot.

Right, top: Scimitar production. This photograph shows XD233 under construction, an airframe retained by the manufacturers as a static test specimen, principally to demonstrate and confirm the Scimitar's fatigue life.

minimum-speed control during catapult launches and deck landings.

The first Type 544, WT854, was flown on 20 January 1956 from the Aircraft and Armament Experimental Establishment at Boscombe Down by the Chief Test Pilot, Mike Lithgow. An accident occurred during spinning trials in which the RN test pilot was killed. After various discussions and wind-tunnel trials, it was decided to invert the tailplane, i.e. change it from dihedral to anhedral—the story goes that this was suggested by an apprentice employed by Supermarine—thereby giving the pilot improved longitudinal control. Following further successful trials, an initial production batch was manufactured, and these aircraft were delivered to 700X Squadron, the IFTU based at RNAS Ford (HMS *Peregrine*), in August 1957. The first operational squadron, 803 NAS, was formed in June 1958 at RNAS Lossiemouth.

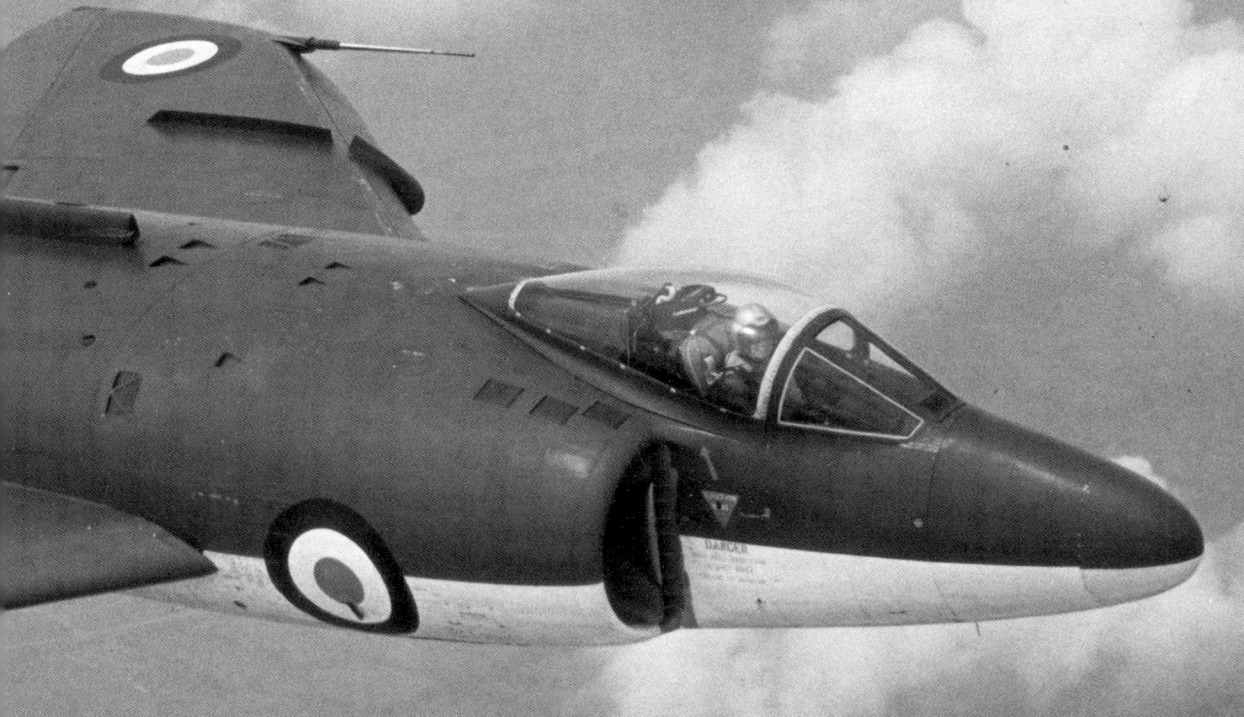

FROM THE COCKPIT

THE Scimitar and Sea Vixen were the first big jets to enter service in the Royal Navy, and the first to have specially built aircraft simulator trainers for the crews. The simulators, which were housed in a large mobile caravan parked close by the Training Squadron, were capable of reproducing standard flight procedures, of imitating aircraft manœuvres in all planes, and of creating every conceivable emergency the crews were likely to encounter and giving guidance as to how such an emergency could be coped with in order to make a safe recovery aboard ship or ashore. The Scimitar Simulator at Lossiemouth was run by Lieutenant Colin Casperd.

While serving as an instructor in 738 Squadron at Lossiemouth, I decided, as I was approaching the time for reappointment to another squadron, to have a word with Lieutenant-Commander 'Jock' Mancais, the CO of 736 Squadron, the Scimitar Operational Flying School, with a request that I be permitted to familiarise myself on the fighter. 'Jock' was very amenable to the idea, particularly as there was a slack period with the OFS students going through the conversion course; moreover, there happened to be a Lieutenant-Commander (G)(P), a gunnery specialist, who also wanted to check out on the aircraft. It was agreed that the pair of us would make up a very short course consisting of seven flights apiece. Each of us, after making five 'flights' in the simulator, was then briefed for his first flight in the 'Big Jet'; each would fly five familiarisation flights followed by a couple of general handling and in-flight refuelling sorties.

The briefing officer walked me out to the aircraft, and as I stood in front of this monstrous jet fighter, I thought to myself, 'Doust, you may have bitten off more than you can chew!' The aircraft stood well above me, and the two huge circular intakes were rather overpowering and intimidating. Then, with a 'Let's go', the briefing officer took me around the outside check, pointing out where there might have been defects; the worst were usually minute fuel and hydraulic oil leaks, for which the aircraft was well known. The climb up to the cockpit was straightforward and, before entering, I looked over the upper surfaces of the fighter for any possible defects, and then checked that the ejection seat safety pins were in their 'ground safe' positions. The briefing officer then discussed the cockpit with me before I strapped myself into the seat. Once I was happy he gave me a squeeze of the left shoulder and I was on my own—although, if I *did* have any problem, of course, I could talk to him via a radio cable link.

The Scimitar had a relatively large cockpit when compared with that of the old Hawker Sea Hawk jet fighter. All the controls were readily to hand and the flight instruments were all well situated, with the six basic instruments—artificial horizon, air speed indicator, altimeter, compass, turn-and-slip indicator and rate-of-climb indicator—placed immediately in front of the control column. There was a good all-round view from the cockpit except in the six o'clock position immediately astern, where it was blocked by the top of the ejection seat.

The pre-start-up cockpit checks were simple and straightforward. Starting each engine (generally speaking, the port powerplant first) was accomplished by means of a Palouste low-pressure air starter—in effect, a miniature jet engine mounted on a small external trolley with a hose connected to the aircraft's engine starter. Once connected, the Palouste would idle until the pilot pressed the starter button in the cockpit, whereupon it would accelerate to full power. The pilot opened the high-pressure fuel cock at the same time, the ignitors in the engine would then crackle away, lighting up the fuel spray mist in the jet burner tubes, and quite quickly the engine would reach idling rpm and the Palouste would automatically cut out and run down to idle. The groundcrew would then switch the starting hose to the other engine and the same procedure would be carried out. Once both engines were idling properly and oil pressures, jet-pipe temperature and rpm were all checked, the wings were spread and checks were carried out to ensure that the locking pins had gone 'home' properly, that the leading- and trailing-edge flaps were lowered and that 'blow' was exiting over the flaps. Then the controls were checked for full and free movement, the chocks were waved away and, on a land base, taxi clearance was requested from the Air Traffic Control tower. A temporary stop was made at the runway threshold in order to carry out final take-off checks, including take-off flap and 'blow' switches 'on', and then line-up and take-off were requested from the tower.

The fastest jet fighter that I had flown to date was the Hawker Hunter Mk 4 at RAF Kemble while on the Flying Instructor's Course at RAF Little Rissington. It was a 'clean' aircraft, that is, it had no wing pylons or drop tanks, and it took off like a rocket: before I had really recovered, the fighter was at 15,000 feet going almost vertical with its undercarriage still down! So I was a little apprehensive about the performance of the Scimitar.

Once on the runway and lined up I opened the throttles to full power and checked the engine instruments for the correct readings. There was a noticeable thrust in the seat and back—the Scimitar's acceleration was extremely high—and very quickly I was airborne and busily retracting the landing gear and flaps as well as selecting 'blow' 'off'. Then I settled down to the climbing speed of 400 knots and within three to five minutes the fighter was at 35,000 feet, punching a hole on its way to heaven, at which altitude the cruise was around 0.8–0.9 Mach: the climbing performance was fantastic! However, the *handling* performance at high altitude was far from what I expected, and I quickly learned that above the clouds the Scimitar had to be flown with care.

During general handling at altitude the aircraft was rather heavy and somewhat sluggish, but it

This spread: Four Scimitars from 736 Naval Air Squadron cruise close to their base, RNAS Lossiemouth, 1964. This unit, serving as the OFS2 training squadron, flew Scimitars from summer 1959 until spring 1965.

SCIMITAR

Above: Close in to 804 Squadron's Scimitars during a pass over the 1962 Farnborough Air Show.
Below: ADDLs (Aerodrome Dummy Deck Landings) with 736 Squadron at Lossiemouth in 1961.
Right: Top o' the loop: a remarkable photograph showing aircraft of 736 Squadron in 'Box Four' formation, practising close to RNAS Lossiemouth for the 1962 Farnborough Air Show.

began to come into its own at about 25,000 feet or below. When performing aerobatics at 10–15,000 feet it responded very well. On returning to the airfield one might carry out several circuits with touch-and-go landings, and then the final landing was made. The aircraft was a delight to fly in the landing circuit, and I could put it exactly where I wanted it. I had to watch the fuel very carefully as the Scimitar was very definitely of the gas-guzzling persuasion: my first flight lasted just 45 minutes before I was down to minimum fuel.

Good aerodynamic braking could be achieved by holding the nose high; then, as the speed fell off, the nose was gently lowered and main-wheel braking was applied. The actual touch-down tended to be firm. Wheel braking was good and positive on most runways and in most conditions, including hard-packed snow, though not on icy surfaces.

The airfield circuit was much the same size as that made by any other jet, but I had to ensure that the 'blow' switch was 'on': without 'blow' over the flaps, control would be lost below 175 knots. As the final approach was made, I felt as if I were sitting out on the nose of the fighter. A fairly high attitude was maintained through to touch-down, and kept until I was airborne again. Taxying

TEN

ELEVEN

called for some care, because the aircraft could easily reach dangerously high taxi speeds.

On my sixth flight I had the opportunity to carry out in-flight refuelling. The Sea Vixen tanker aircraft towed a hose-and-drogue astern of a wing-mounted refuelling pod at 250 knots. The Scimitar's refuelling probe was installed in the starboard top side of the aircraft's nose cone, just forward of the cockpit, so it was quite an easy matter to steer it into the drogue. One approached the tanker after clearance from its crew with a few knots' overtaking speed in hand, along the line of the drogue and hose. Contact was usually made with a resounding *thunk*, and then the lights on the rear of the pod and the drogue indicated that fuel was flowing. In training sessions, approximately 500 pounds of fuel would be transferred from the tanker. Once the transfer had been completed, the Scimitar pilot throttled back slightly to disengage from the drogue and drop astern along the line of the hose, then a smooth right-hand turn was made away from the tanker, and finally he accelerated to come alongside, level with the tanker, to give the 'thumbs up' that all was well. Radio communication was kept to a minimum—which would be the normal practice while flying near or over enemy territory. With his refuelling completed, the Scimitar pilot resumed his sortie.

Although now qualified on the Scimitar, I was in October 1960 appointed to 764 (Advanced Weaponry) Squadron, where the Air Warfare Instructors and the Sea Hawk OFS1 students went for their 'Swept Wing' in-flight training prior to moving on, to either the Scimitar or the Sea Vixen OFS Part 2 flight training. In the summer of 1962,

This spread: Scimitar refuelling in flight from a Sea Vixen tanker, as described by the author. The fuel was transferred via the 'hose and drogue' system fed from a 'buddy' pod on the tanker aircraft's wing pylon. Scimitars were also themselves frequently employed as tanker aircraft; indeed, 800B Flight was established for this very purpose, extending the capabilities of the new Buccaneer strike bomber when it first entered service.

towards the end of my tour with 764 Squadron, I took the AWI course, passed, and thereby became the only dual-qualified QFI and AWI in the Royal Navy. I then moved 'next door' into the hangar where 736 (Scimitar Training) Squadron was located and took up my duties as an instructor. The new OFS2 students, apart from familiarising themselves on the Scimitar, would undertake training sorties consisting of air-to-air gunnery using camera guns and including a live session on a air-towed banner, ground-attack exercises using rocket projectiles, 30mm cannon strafing, and dive and low-level bombing using 25-pound practice bombs. They would then fly FAC (Forward Air Control) and navigation sorties, undertake some night flying and carry out intensive ADDLs (Aerodrome Dummy Deck Landings) before being appointed to a front-line squadron.

During my time in 736, the Admiralty decided that, because the trial catapult was being under-used at RAE Bedford, Scimitar and Sea Vixen OFS students would all be given three catapult launches, so that they could learn the loading and launch procedures. The RN Flight Deck Trials Unit was

THIRTEEN

SCIMITAR

based at Bedford, formerly known as RAF Thurleigh. It was originally a farm, owned by my foster father's brother in the period when I was evacuated during World War II. When the airfield was built, it became a base for B-17 Flying Fortresses of the US Eighth Air Force. After the war, the Ministry of Defence created a second Royal Aircraft Establishment there, for in-depth trials for both civil and

Above: A Scimitar towards the end of its career: XD215, in the markings of 764B Flight—with an identical fin emblem to 736 Squadron's but with revised call-signs—photographed while being used for deck-handler training aboard HMS *Hermes* in 1966. Opposite: The same aircraft while on charge to 736 Squadron a year earlier, displayed in the aircraft park at RAF Biggin Hill.. Below: XD226 (736 NAS) having come to grief on Lossiemouth's main runway following the collapse of its nosewheel, April 1963.

FROM THE COCKPIT

military aircraft. It was also used by the British Overseas Airways Corporation as a training airfield for their heavy jet airliners. One of the recent installations at Bedford was the steam catapult, built by Brown Brothers of Edinburgh, for naval aircraft trials.

Accordingly, I flew south from Lossiemouth one morning, accompanied by three Scimitar students.

After landing, they were all given a catapult loading lecture and then, together with the instructor, who went first, they all received three satisfactory launches. The Scimitar was loaded in an odd way: when tensioned for the launch, the aircraft was pulled down on to its retractable tail skid with the nose high in the air so that the aircraft was in the correct flying attitude. On board a carrier, take-off

FIFTEEN

OH! FOR ANOTHER SCIMITAR TOUR!
Lieutenant Ian Frenz

As a 'plane crazy' teenager I had been thrilled and awed by these potent and lethal looking machines thundering across my Perthshire home. It did not seem very long after surviving Wings Training and OFS1 that I found myself actually rocketing airborne from RNAS Lossiemouth in a mighty Scimitar displaying all the aplomb of a misguided missile.

The 736 Squadron Scimitar Course consisted of sixty-five tightly packed hours on the aircraft plus eight to ten flown on the Hunter T Mk 8 used for checks and instrument training. Transition from the Hunter to the Scimitar required different techniques in circuit work: a back-of-the-drag curve approach and a high nose-up landing attitude frequently resulted in the duty runway LCN (surface strength) being rigorously tested by beginners!

On completion of my course in August 1963 I spent eighteen months initially with 800 Squadron embarked on *Ark Royal* and commanded by Lieutenant-Commander D. F. Mills prior to being reappointed to 803 Squadron at Lossiemouth, the CO then being Lieutenant-Commander N. J. P. Mills, later succeeded by Lieutenant-Commander P. G. Newman. In November 1964 I transferred to 800B Flight as the fourth pilot on the In Flight Refuelling Unit, to be embarked on HMS *Eagle*, hoping desperately to escape from the clutches of the Pilot's Appointer and gain another tour on Scimitars. Throughout this entire period I had received excellent training in day carrier operations, dive bombing, rocketing, strafing, air-to-air combat, Sidewinder and Bullpup missiles and in-flight refuelling as well as participating in major military exercises and air shows. The Scimitar certainly gave one varied flying roles, and I rapidly—and at times frighteningly—began to understand what the term 'naval aviator' meant!

I found the Scimitar's cockpit to be roomy and well laid out for that era, although when LABS and other equipment was added the view could be impaired. All-round visibility was very good, although, being of modest stature, I required my seat fully raised for deck landing. The aircraft handled responsively throughout the speed range, it had plenty of power, it made plenty of noise and it used plenty of sky! It was seldom a boring machine: with hydraulic systems operating at 4,000psi, failures were not uncommon and in high ambient temperatures spurious warnings caused the Central Warning Panel to light up like a juke box displaying the full menu or an equally appalling selection of impending disasters, inducing an added adrenaline surge when halfway down the catapult! Our 800 Squadron French Navy exchange pilot *Capitaine de Corvette* Michel Borney, when asked his opinion of the Scimitar, replied in his inimitable French manner, 'Ah! The bells they ring and the lights they flash, but she flies!' Serviceability could be a nightmare, and our FAA maintenance personnel displayed great skill and professionalism working in frequently unpleasant conditions under much pressure. Without them I could never have had so many unforgettable experiences.

Unfortunately, the Appointer caught up with me near Hong Kong and my last flight in the aircraft involved the delivery of an 800B machine to the China Aeronautical Engineering Company at Kai Tak airfield, Hong Kong, where naval aircraft could be refurbished should a carrier be operating in that area. This allowed me the rare opportunity to fly an aircraft with no pylons or underwing tanks and in the cool temperature and strong wind conditions my 'clean' Scimitar shot off *Eagle*'s big catapult like a paper dart! In an amazingly short period of time I found myself close to Mach 1 and covered in a cloud of condensation for a low farewell run past that great warship, then on to the CO's wing for a formation GCA into Kai Tak, where I very sadly said goodbye to my big beautiful Scimitar.

Thinking of the Scimitar will always give me great feelings of nostalgia, despite its operational shortcomings. It was an exciting aircraft—and one that I was proud to fly.

Below: Sub-Lieutenant Ian Frenz in his 'office', 800B Flight, HMS *Eagle*, 1964.

Below: Halcyon days: 800 (foreground) and 807 Squadron Scimitars at RNAS Lossiemouth, August 1959.

Above: 'Roller' practice—no catapult strop, no hook down—by XD214, 803 Squadron, HMS *Victorious*, January 1961.

flap was selected with the 'blow' switch set to 'on', the Flight Deck Officer (FDO) then waved his Green Flag, and when the pilot was happy that he had full power he dropped his hand in a salute and the FDO brought his Green Flag down in the direction of the launch. The actual launch speed was based upon the wind-over-deck (WOD) and the aircraft's all-up weight (AUW), the necessary calculations always being made by the Lieutenant-Commander (Flying) in the carrier and then passed on to the Flight Deck Engineer Officer (FDEO), who in turn calculated the steam pressure required to reach the end speed for the aircraft's AUW and the WOD conditions. In most cases the WOD was about 30 knots on board a carrier, but ashore the endspeed off the catapult would be much higher because the catapult would not, as it were, be moving. The launch was made in the region of 160–170 knots indicated air speed. (Of course, on board a carrier steaming directly into the wind at, say 20 knots, and with a WOD of, say 30 knots, the actual velocity imparted by the catapult to the aircraft at launch would be 50 knots less than the IAS.)

During one of the launches at Bedford, the instructor thought that he was going to have an accident with one of his students. This young pilot

SUPERMARINE SCIMITAR F. Mk 1
COCKPIT CONTROLS AND EQUIPMENT

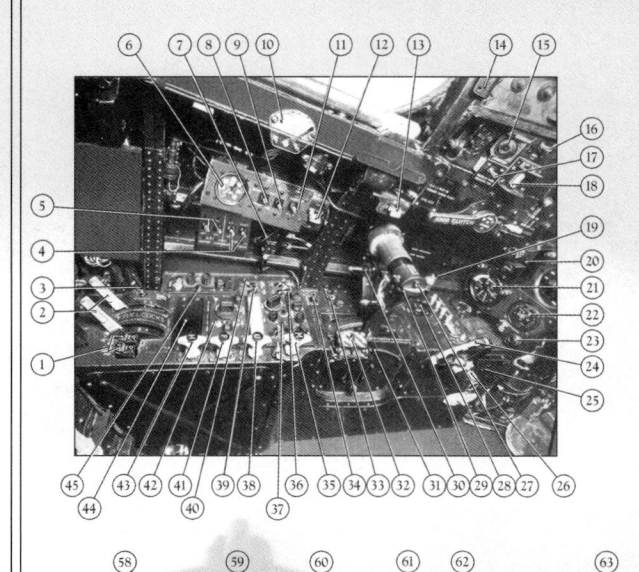

1. Engine ignition circuit breakers (two)
2. LP fuel cocks (two)
3. External intercom switch
4. Blue Silk control switches (two)
5. GPI control switches (two)
6. Emergency system hydraulic pressure gauge
7. Windscreen de-icing cock
8. VP azimuth/elevation switch
9. VP meter sensitivity switch
10. Hood rails locked indicator
11. Standby UHF emergency P to Tx switch
12. IFF, ARN 21–EP, EL fusing inverter switch
13. High intensity light switch
14. Position for LABS controller
15. Telebriefing connected light
16. Telebriefing call switch
17. Radar ranging presentation switch
18. Blown flaps switch
19. Target reject switch
20. Undercarriage pushbuttons (two)
21. Wheel brakes triple pressure gauge
22. Undercarriage position indicator
23. Hook down light
24. Hood jettison handle
25. Hood jettison handle safety pin stowage
26. Hood jettison handle safety pin
27. P to T pushbutton
28. Engine starting push buttons (two)
29. Airbrakes switch
30. Engine relight pushbuttons (two)
31. Throttles friction lever
32. Duplicate trim switch
33. Autostabiliser switch
34. Rudder trim switch
35. Emergency hydraulic system master control handle
36. UHF set selector and standby power
37. Radio controller
38. Undercarriage emergency handle
39. Standby UHF channel selector
40. Radio altimeter switch
41. Flaps emergency handle
42. IFF controller
43. Hook emergency handle
44. Position for SIF controller
45. Tacan controller
46. Voltmeter and alternative position
47. Radio altimeter height band selector
48. Hood clutch lever
49. GPI variation setting control
50. Airbrakes magnetic indicator
51. Flaps selector lever
52. Hood selector lever
53. Flap override switch
54. Cockpit emergency lights switch
55. Arrester hook selector switch
56. External stores jettison switch
57. Port 'attention getter' light
58. Accelerometer
59. Feel simulator one failed magnetic indicator
60. Radio altimeter limit lights (three)
61. Parking brake handle
62. Gun sight
63. Oxygen flow magnetic indicator
64. Tacan indicator
65. Air to air refuelling master switch
66. Oil pressure magnetic indicators (two)
67. Green Salad or Violet Picture indicator
68. Starboard 'attention getter' light
69. Drop tank fuel transfer indicator
70. Engine rpm indicators (two)
71. Summation fuel contents gauge
72. Jpt indicators (two)
73. Artificial horizon standby power switch
74. High intensity light
75. Fuel contents gauges (eight)
76. Booster pump failure warning lights (eight)
77. Fuel pressure magnetic indicators (two)
78. Cockpit altimeter
79. Oxygen contents gauge
80. Fuel balancing retrim switch
81. Booster pump failure selector switch
82. De-icing magnetic indicator
83. Guard for 'all armament' trigger switch
84. Tailplane and aileron trim switch
85. Camera switch
86. Valve 'B' failure switch
87. Fuel flowmeter
88. No 1 inverter fail magnetic indicator
89. Flight instrument reset switch
90. Drop tanks selector switch
91. Jpt control switches (two) 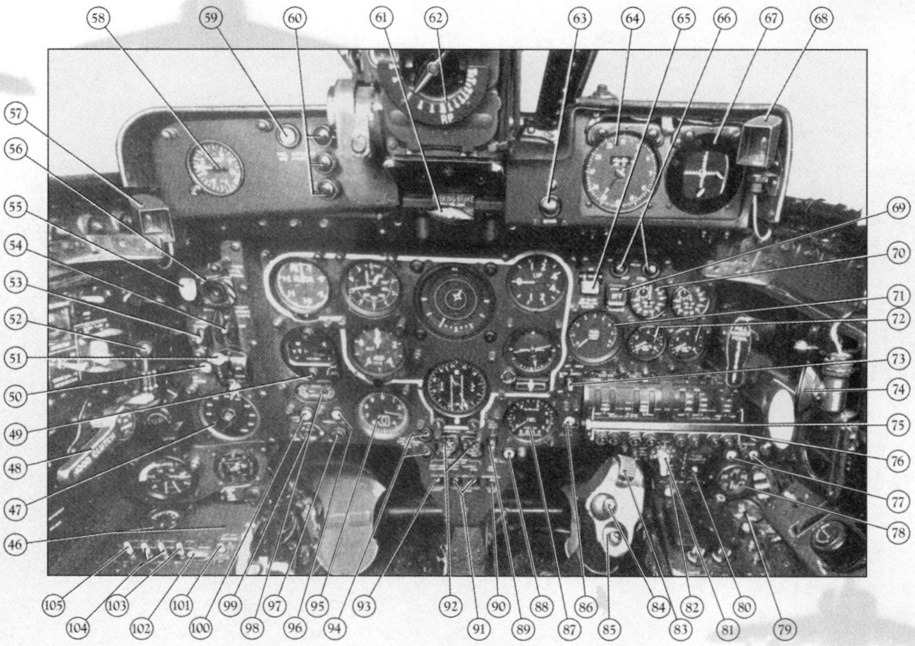
92. Nos 1 and 2 systems hydraulic pressure gauges (two)
93. Drop tanks fuel override switch
94. Take-off safe trim magnetic indicators (two)
95. Radio altimeter indicator
96. Fuselage flaps indicator
97. 'Blown flaps on' light
98. Trailing edge flaps position indicator
99. Tailplane position indicator
100. Leading edge flaps locked magnetic indicator
101. Battery isolation switch
102. Fuel master switch
103. Pressure head heater switch
104. Engine selection switches (two)
105. Instrument early start switch
106. Recuperator failure magnetic indicator
107. Standard warning panel switches (three)
108. Firebell normal/off switch
109. Cockpit manual vent
110. GGS practice switch
111. Cockpit lights master switch
112. Cockpit general lights dimmer switch
113. Starboard louvre
114. Ancillary lights off/dimmer switch
115. Position for target towing master switch
116. Gunsight dive bomb selector switch
117. Stowage for seat pins
118. Navigation lights switch
119. Navigation lights bright/dim switch
120. Formation lights switch
121. Hood seal manual inflation cock
122. Ventilated suit temperature control
123. Ventilated suit flow control.
124. Wing-and-nose locked magnetic indicator
125. Carrier/airfield switch
126. Anti-'g' on/off cock
127. Ice detector test switch
128. Fire detection test switch
129. Wingfold control lever
130. Oxygen regulator
131. Flowmeter specific gravity compensator
132. Windscreen demisting switch
133. Cabin air master switch
134. Cabin air temperature control
135. Ice detection and engine anti-icing switch
136. GGS controller
137. Emergency oxygen handle
138. Stores jettison pylon switches (three)
139. Detachable panel for change of role
140. RP switch
141. Radar failure magnetic indicator
142. Radar on/off switch
143. RP selector switch
144. Master armament selector switch
145. Stowage for ejection seat main and secondary firing safety pins (two)
146. Fire-extinguisher pushbuttons (two) 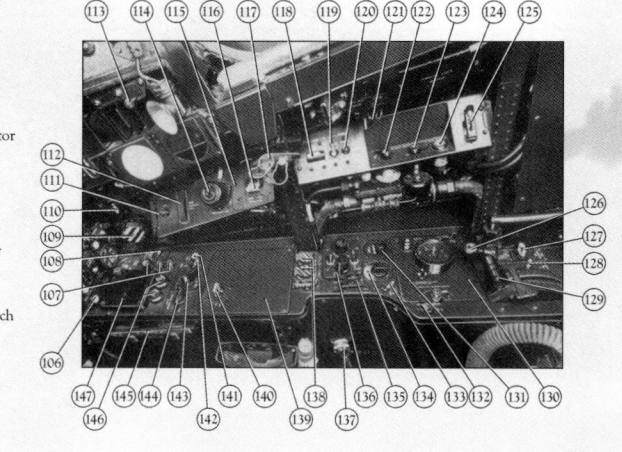
147. Standard warning panel switches (two)

PHOTOGRAPHS AND INFORMATION COURTESY SOLENT SKY AIR MUSEUM

FROM THE COCKPIT

Above: XD215 undertaking launch testing as part of the CofA Release Trials aboard *Ark Royal* in the summer of 1957.
Right: The catapult strop falls away as a Scimitar is 'squirted'.

stood not more than about 5 feet 3 inches in his stockinged feet. When his aircraft was tensioned, he appeared to be seated normally, but as the aircraft was launched he disappeared from view, and as the jet left the end of the catapult it reared into a very steep, nose-up attitude and the left wing dropped. The aircraft proceeded around the airfield in a left-hand turn at an altitude of a couple of hundred feet and then landed safely. Everybody at the catapult, including the instructor, just stood there wondering what was going to happen: the aircraft could easily have slid sideways into the ground and exploded, but somehow our young naval aviator managed to grab control of the jet to make a normal touch-down.

Below: XD219, lacking its undercarriage doors and outer wing panels, undertakes wet-runway trials at RAE Farnborough in 1971. By this time the Scimitar had long been out of front-line service.

NINETEEN

SINGLE-THROTTLE TECHNIQUE

Captain Alan Leahy CBE DSC

When the Scimitar came into service it was a step up in size, capability and complexity after the Sea Hawk and the Hunter. Its performance far exceeded that of any aircraft that was in British service at that time. When I was appointed CO of 803 Squadron in December 1959, Scimitar flying hours were like gold dust as the maintenance/flying hours ratio was badly out of balance. As an example, the fuel system was prone to leaks (if usually small ones). One Chief Petty Officer, an expert in curing these leaks, was convinced that when the aircraft was built the first step was to hang a particularly important fuel union from the roof by a piece of string and then build the aircraft all round it.

Once you were confident that you had understood all the briefings that you had been given, things were not as bad as you thought they might be. Start-up was never a problem, unless you diverted to an airfield with no air starter. Taxying was not a problem, either ashore or on deck. It did not take too long to get used to the way that the Scimitar would charge into the air. Then you discovered that it was fun to fly. Aerobatics were aided by well-balanced controls, and slow rolls—or 'twinkle rolls'—were easy. The fast rate of roll meant that it could be difficult to stop it where you wanted to, and I would never do one as part of a low-level display. Too scary!

There has been a lot of talk about the Scimitar and its 'controlled crash' kind of landing. By flying down the glide slope as indicated by the mirror sight, you could guarantee that at the approach speed you would land at the correct spot—which is the kind of place you want to land on a carrier. Yes, it crunched down but I never heard of a Scimitar being damaged that way. With a deck landing, the crunch, followed by rapid deceleration, made for a very happy feeling. The worse the sea state the more difficult the ride down the glide slope, but there was another hazard which often occurred, normally associated with a calm sea. The Scimitar required more than twenty knots of wind over the deck, and if there was little or no natural wind then the ship had to get up speed in order to achieve the right wind speed over the deck. This gave rise to the hot gases from the funnel rising into the glide path on the final approach to the deck—which was very disconcerting the first time you experienced it because the Scimitar would suddenly lose speed and increase its rate of descent. If no correction was applied you stood a good chance of hitting the round-down, and if too much power was applied you could zoom past the arrester wires and have to come round for another try. There was a solution to this and it was known as the 'single throttle technique'.

The twin Rolls-Royce Avons were very responsive engines and could deliver large amounts of power quickly—not quite what you wanted at a critical stage of the landing! When you got settled on the glide slope you had a datum with both throttles at the same setting, and any small divergence up or down could be adjusted by moving a single throttle up or down and then bringing the power back to the original state (a method used by many auto-throttle systems). One landing on board HMS *Ark Royal*, with 45 knots over the deck (which caused severe turbulence from the island structure), resulted in the hook tearing out a sodium light on the round-down. Unfortunately the pilot, Lieutenant-Commander Hefford, mentioned in the accident report that he had been using the 'single-throttle technique'. The result was that some bright spark, who had probably never flown a Scimitar let alone deck-landed one, convinced Their Lordships that this was a 'bad thing' and the practice was banned. This meant that you could not teach it . . . although, if you used it, who could tell?

Below: 'Everything down' and undercarriage oleos at full stretch, the first production Scimitar, XD212, demonstrates the aircraft's landing attitude. This particular aircraft was used extensively for in-flight refuelling trials and ended its days with 736 NAS at Lossiemouth.

FROM THE COCKPIT

Top left: An 800 Squadron Scimitar on board *Ark Royal* in mid-1963 displaying come interesting markings. The '7' in the call-sign on the nose and nosewheel door is an adaptation of the figure '6' from the aircraft's earlier identity as '106', and note also the winged bomb and pilot's name painted on the engine casing.
Top right: On board *Ark Royal* at about the same time, with a US Navy E-1B Tracer cross-decking in the background.
Above: An 804 Squadron Scimitar is launched from *Hermes*, 1961.
Below: Scimitars of 803 Squadron take off for a display at RNAS Yeovilton, June 1964.

The CO of the Naval Unit had been watching and wanted know what on earth had happened, and once we had the pilot to ourselves it became apparent that he had been an extremely lucky man. As the aircraft had started down the catapult, his rudder bars had broken away from him and moved fully forward: they had not been locked properly. At the same time he had slid down and forward in his ejection seat, and, being so short in stature, could

TWENTY-ONE

THE ESSENTIAL THRILL

Lieutenant-Commander Phil Cardew

I enjoyed my first take-off enormously: compared to other aircraft I have flown, it was quite definitely the most exciting. I would say my best moments were when flying low-level strikes with Doppler navigation. The permitted IAS gave one the essential thrill. For deck landing the arrival was precise and easily controlled. The Vixen could easily float over the wires but it would flare beautifully on the runway. The strong point with the Scimitar was its crosswind limitation. Not many, if any, could match that. The weak point was in allowing the nose to drop on deck landing; that would cause a wire miss every time, if not worse. High up it was a dog, but it certainly arrived there quickly—530 knots converting to Mach 0.83. I seem to remember that down low it was sensational. Surrounded by its attendant puffball of condensation, it looked good too.

There were several incidents that caused both embarrassment and a few breathless moments. Of these, I choose 1962 when engaged in exercises with the Sixth Fleet. My mission was HiCap and the 'enemy' were, as I recollect, Vigilantes from USS *Forrestal*. I was leading a section at 40,000 feet being vectored in to a quarter attack. We were 'bounced', and in my enthusiasm to obtain camera-gun footage 'overcooked' both the Scimitar's and my own capabilities. I spun from 40,000 to 20,000 feet. Reminding myself that as the Squadron QFI I had carried out Hunter spinning a year previously with a well-known test pilot, I tried most of the tricks he had taught me and happily it worked out and I re-joined the fray. My No 2 was most impressed and unhappily expressed his comments in the hearing of Freddy Mills the CO. Freddy promptly assembled the Squadron pilots and stated that it was all very well for Philip to spin since he was the QFI, but he, Freddy, would not tolerate another of us doing the same. Exit left one astonished QFI.

While embarked in *Hermes* in 1963 near Penang in the Malacca Strait, I was launched at maximum catapult weight with a light wind on a hot day. My wing blow failed and the aircraft pitched up dramatically and then rolled right. Fortunately those big engines pushed me out of trouble. FLYCO were very impressed and thought I had lost it. They were not alone in that thought! A further wing blow incident occurred later at Tengah. My left engine flamed out on the way back from live firing up-country. I made a careful single-engine approach, fortunately with height in hand. This time the 'blow' was 'on', despite being selected 'off'. I landed okay but breathing heavily with full-power-plus on the good engine.

In 1962, 803 Squadron commenced flight refuelling ('buddy/buddy') practice off the Italian coast. I believe we left three hoses and drogues on Mount Etna whilst practising the art before being issued with the more flexible hose. I, however, managed to bring back one drogue firmly attached to my probe for the subsequent deck landing. It was embarrassing, and Tommy Leece, our CO, summoned the Squadron for a short and very sharp talk about our skill or lack of it!

Comparing with USN aircraft, they were much more advanced year for year, but their operations and direction were not a patch on ours. They preferred to be directed by the RN in cross-operations. Developments? Reducing parasite and form drag.

I would do it all over again—but only on post-Mod. 494 aircraft!

Above: Lieutenant Cardew cruises in his Scimitar. Phil served with both 736 NAS (SP) and 803 NAS (QFI).
Right: The aftermath of an over-energetic Scimitar in-flight refuelling disengagement, similar to that mentioned in this article.

FROM THE COCKPIT

Above: Another view of XD215 of the Royal Navy Test Squadron on board *Ark Royal* during trials in 1957. This aircraft went on to enjoy a hard-working and varied career, serving with 803 and 736 Squadrons and ending its days with 764B.
Below: On board HMS *Victorious*, an 803 Squadron Scimitar is readied for launch from the starboard catapult, September 1958. De Havilland Sea Venoms of 893 NAS are parked forward. The area-ruled 'wasp waist' of the Scimitar is especially evident in this photograph.

hardly see over the cockpit coaming. To this day nobody really knows why he did not crash.

By mid-1963 I had been reappointed as the Air Warfare Instructor with 800 Squadron aboard *Ark Royal*, which was at the time on deployment in the Far East. Towards the end of July 1963, therefore, I was flown out to Singapore by RAF Britannia, via El

TWENTY-THREE

Left: In high-drag mode, Scimitar tanker XD277 of 800B Flight approaches HMS *Eagle* for a touch-down, spring 1965.
Below: Closer: XD243 of 800 NAS approaches *Ark Royal*'s round-down, 1963.
Far right: XD214 of 803 Squadron takes the wire aboard HMS *Hermes* (top); and XD333 of the same unit is seen in a sequence of three images being guided into the deck park. Notice, from the shadows, that *Hermes*, having turned into the wind for landing-on, on completion immediately resumes course.

Adem in the Sahara, Aden and Gan. Night had already closed in when the Britannia landed and I was bussed up to the wardroom at the naval base just in time for dinner, and early to bed.

Ark Royal was at this time still steaming north from Fremantle, having paid a visit to the west coast of Australia, and I would join her via HMNZS *Otago*, which would be exercising with the carrier as her planeguard. Once alongside the carrier, I, together with my luggage, was transferred across by breeches buoy into the arms of the waiting CO, SP and AWI. After a quick meeting with the Captain and Commander (Air), I settled into my cabin, and then went below to the wardroom to meet the Air Group, have beer or two, and then dinner and off to bed for well-earned night's sleep.

The following day I changed into flight gear and climbed up to the flight deck, to be met by the Squadron Line Chief and informed that one of the Squadron pilots—a friend and a former student, as it happened—had crashed into the sea: he had apparently pulled out too low from a rocket-firing attack and hit the sea, his Scimitar had exploded and he had been killed. The CO, SP and Commander

TWENTY-FOUR

(Air) all said that I did not have to fly in view of the tragic accident, but I wanted to fly and salute my friend's passing.

The start-up and catapult-loading went as planned, final cockpit checks were carried out and, making sure that the 'blow' was selected 'on', I dropped my right hand to indicate to the Launch Officer that I was ready to go. I sat back firmly in the ejection seat with my head braced against the seat's head-rest and the control column held firmly with the right elbow jammed into my stomach, thus preventing the it from moving backwards as the aircraft lurched forward. With a solid thumb I was airborne, accelerating away from the carrier, raising the landing gear and flaps and selecting the 'blow' 'off.'

After climbing to 25,000 feet and turning towards Singapore, I obtained a weather report from the Singapore Met. Centre, which gave fog over most of the island though patchy at RAF Tengah. In fact, it was relatively clear at Tengah, and so a couple of circuits were carried out there and then a return course was made for the carrier. Following three touch-and-go's on the flight deck, the hook was lowered and a good arrested landing was made, catching the target No 2 wire . . .

Following a carrier landing, the Scimitar would roll backwards automatically owing to the tension in the wire and the hook would be disengaged. The Flight Handler indicated 'Hook up' and the pilot was then passed on to the next handler further along the deck, who indicated 'Raise flaps and fold the

Left: The salvage of XD239, forced to ditch in shallow water off Aden on 22 May 1963 after the pilot, Sub-Lieutenant Legg, reported hydraulics problems. Below: Brake failure while taxying resulted in Lieutenant D. S. MacIntyre's XD269 veering off the flight deck, 803 Squadron, *Victorious*, July 1961. The aircraft soon slipped over the side completely, but fortunately the pilot was uninjured. Opposite bottom: Hydraulic failure deprived Lieutenant (E) M. G. Griffin (807 Squadron) of brakes when landing at RAF Khormaksar, Aden, in September 1961 and his aircraft, XD282, ended up on the beach beyond the end of the runway.

wings'. This handler then passed the landing pilot on to the next handler, who guided him into the forward aircraft park, 'chocked' his wheels and positioned a couple of tie-down chains before giving the visual order to shut down . . .

As I climbed out, I glanced up at FLYCO, and there were all my Squadron pals, standing there, grinning and giving the 'thumbs up'—a happy band of warriors!

Flying the Scimitar in the carrier circuit was found to be easy. Once on the mirror landing sight glidepath, the aircraft's attitude was maintained by the control column and the rate of descent was controlled by the throttles. The correct attitude and airspeed were easy to fly because there was both a steady aural tone in the earphones when on speed and a physical display of the 'doughnut-and-chevrons' that also let the pilot know whether he was on speed, too fast or too slow. The view over the nose was excellent, offering a clear picture of the flight deck and landing sight. As soon as the pilot hit the deck, whether he was arrested or missed the wires, he automatically selected air brakes 'in' and full power so that in the event of a 'bolter' the engines were at maximum blast as he departed to make another attempt . . .

After checking back into the Line Office and signing the Aircraft Logbook Form A700, I proceeded to the Briefing Room to be debriefed and to discuss various points that had arisen during the sortie. It was a great feeling to be back 'in the saddle' again!

SCIMITAR EJECTIONS

Unit/base	Date	Aircraft	Pilot	Remarks
A&AEE/Boscombe Down	05/07/55	VX138	Lt-Cdr A. Rickell	Type 525. Aircraft failed to recover from spin. Pilot fatally injured.
807 NAS/Lossiemouth	10/11/59	XD281	Lt N. Grier-Rees	Aircraft entered steep dive at 20,000ft/440kts following hydraulic failure. Pilot suffered limb injuries owing to 'flailing' following ejection.
803 NAS/*Victorious*	06/02/60	XD238	Lt-Cdr Davies	Aircraft diverted from ship, ran out of fuel 400yds short of Lossiemouth duty runway. Pilot slightly injured.
803 NAS/*Victorious*	09/12/60	XD329	Lt J. W. H. Purvis	Pilot unable to maintain control during high nose attitude off catapult. No injuries.
800 NAS/Lossiemouth	21/07/61	XD264	Lt-Cdr D. Norman	Aircraft crashed 5 miles south of Cullen, northern Scotland, owing to hydraulic failure. Pilot slightly injured.
803 NAS/*Hermes*	11/08/62	XD331	Lt-Cdr B. Willson	Double flame out owing to fuel starvation at 37,000ft. Pilot ejected at 8,000ft, rescued by plane-guard frigate.
736 NAS/Lossiemouth	15/11/62	XD265	Lt-Cdr J. Kennett	Engine fire after bird strike near Dundee. Pilot suffered back injuries.
736 NAS/Lossiemouth	23/11/62	XD262	S/Lt I. Bowden	Pilot error ('blow' not 'on'), aircraft spun on finals. Pilot uninjured.
800 NAS/*Ark Royal*	22/05/63	XD239	S/Lt C. D. Legg	Aircraft diverted to Aden following radio and hydraulic failure, ditched in harbour. Pilot slightly injured.
803 NAS/*Hermes*	20/09/63	XD213	S/Lt A. J. Middleton	Hydraulic failure; one gear leg failed to lower. Pilot uninjured.
800 NAS/*Ark Royal*	28/01/64	XD249	Lt P. E. H. Banfield	Loss of hydraulics. Aircraft crashed into Moray Firth. Pilot uninjured.
ETPS/Farnborough	16/07/64	XD216	Flt Lt B. J. Gartner	Loss of control. Aircraft crashed into English Channel off Wittering, Sussex. Pilot uninjured.
803 NAS/Lossiemouth	28/09/64	XD230	S/Lt P. J. McManus	Hydraulic failure. Aircraft crashed in Moray Firth. Pilot uninjured.
800 NAS/*Eagle*	29/04/65	XD270	Lt I. P. F. Meiklejohn	Double flame out. Aircraft crashed near Aden. Pilot uninjured.
800B Flt/Lossiemouth	15/07/65	XD268	S/Lt A. C. Hill	Crashed 2 miles short of runway in field near Duffus, Morayshire. Pilot slightly injured.
803 NAS/*Ark Royal*	20/09/65	XD223	Lt P. A. Waring	Aircraft on test flight, crashed on finals at RAF Changi owing to engine problem. Pilot injured.
803 NAS/*Ark Royal*	31/12/65	XD318	Lt M. J. Williams	Aircraft ditched in Persian Gulf after fuel problems and missing arrester wires three times. Pilot uninjured.
803 NAS/*Ark Royal*	28/01/66	XD316	S/Lt Z. K. Skrodski	Aircraft pitched up on finals to carrier. Pilot uninjured.
803 NAS/*Ark Royal*	16/02/66	XD250	S/Lt Z. K. Skrodski	Aircraft ditched in Indian Ocean 90nm east of Mombasa after hydraulic failure and fire. Pilot unhurt.
803 NAS/*Ark Royal*	06/04/66	XD277	Lt P. De Souza	Aircraft suffered hydraulic failure and fire warning after take-off from RAF Changi. Pilot slightly injured.

Above: The Martin-Baker Type 4C ejection seat as fitted to the Scimitar.

WEAPONS AND TACTICS

THE Scimitar had five principal missions over the course of its career with the Fleet Air Arm—air-to-air, air-to-ground, forward air control (FAC), nuclear strike and in-flight refuelling

The aircraft's primary air-to-air armament was the 30mm Aden cannon. It was equipped with four of these weapons, each of which was quite capable of blowing apart any known potential enemy aircraft. This gun had been developed from the German 30mm MK 08 cannon used in the Messerschmitt Me 262 twin-jet fighter which had entered service with the Luftwaffe towards the end of World War II. Two cannon were installed beneath each engine intake, and each weapon was supplied with 120 mixed rounds of high-explosive (HE), semi-armour-piercing (SAP) and incendiary.

Aiming and tracking was achieved by the use of a Mk 8 gyro gun sight, which was connected to a radar ranging transmitter and receiver fitted in the front of the aircraft's nose cone. Below 25,000 feet, the Scimitar was easy to steer while tracking a target, and the cannon, when fired, produced a resounding *thud* beneath the cockpit floor. The expended shell cases were collected in a strongbox located behind the guns. The velocity at which these cases were ejected from the breeches had to be seen to be believed: I once watched an Aden fired on a test range, and the cases were projected 800 yards astern of the cannon!

Above: The 30mm Aden Mk 4 cannon, four of which were installed in the Scimitar in the lower intake casings. The weapon had a rate of fire of 1,200 rounds per minute. The Scimitar was the first Fleet Air Arm aircraft to be equipped with these cannon.

Above and below: XD248, an 807 Squadron Scimitar, shows its undersurfaces, the troughs for the quartet of Aden cannon prominent (above) and, probably on the same sortie, fires its 3-inch unguided rocket projectiles (below).

During my time in 736 Squadron at Lossiemouth I was involved in two aircraft trials with the Scimitar, one using podded 2-inch RPs to determine the optimum ground spread for best effect against various targets, and the other with the Sidewinder AAM. The RP trial was handed over to my AWI assistant while I went south to the Aero Medical School for my two-yearly high-altitude tests. When I returned the trial had not been completed, owing to the fact that the aircraft earmarked for the purpose was seriously unserviceable.

The trial concerning the Sidewinder went ahead at RAE Bedford and was a complete success. I flew south and at Bedford a dummy Sidewinder was fitted to the port outboard weapons pylon. The purpose of the trial was to establish what stresses and strains would be placed on the weapon and its wing-mounted carrier during an off-centre arrested landing. Initially the aircraft was placed at half distance from the runway threshold and the arrester wire. The engines were run up to full power, the brakes were released and the Scimitar hurtled into the wire, but nothing untoward happened. The scientists and aero-engineers huddled together, and then after a short while they came over to the jet and re-briefed me to go back to the beginning of the runway in order to catch the arrester wire at a much higher velocity. Although the arrest was, of course, much more violent, nothing could be found wrong with either the missile or its carriage mounting.

Following a further discussion I was then asked to go back to the threshold but to line up on the extreme left-hand edge of the runway. On this occasion the entry speed into the arrester wire was nearly 180 knots, there was an awful bang, the missile came away and flew down the runway with various bits of the carriage mounting and I nearly went through the windscreen, only my ejection seat harness restraining me. The scientists and aero-engineers were by this time all jumping around with joy: they had got what they wanted. When they came on the intercom, I informed them that the aircraft would not be flying again until it had been thoroughly checked over for any structural damage.

Above: Scimitars on display and carrying Sidewinder missiles. Cleared for use by Scimitars in 1963, the Sidewinder homed on to its target's heat source by means of an infra-red seeker in the nose.

I gingerly taxied the aircraft over to the maintenance hangar and then went for a stiff brandy and lunch. By late afternoon the Scimitar was ready and I flew back to Lossiemouth.

The Scimitar could carry up to four Sidewinder anti-aircraft missiles (AAMs), one on each of the four wing pylons. The weapon could be aimed and fired at a target from directly head-on, through the beam and around to the stern, provided that the pilot had a steady tone in his earphones from the seeker head and was within the missile's envelope. The missile was at its best when fired from head-on, because of the increased firing range. As a fighter closed in to the stern position, the firing range was little better than one half to one mile.

It was an excellent air-to-air missile. It was fitted with an expanding-rod warhead which extended to about twenty feet before breaking up and could cut a target in two. Once the rod expanded beyond twenty feet, it broke up into myriad fragments of iron bars, causing considerable damage. The weapon put the Scimitar almost on a par with the Sea Vixen and its Firestreak or Red Top missiles.

ENOUGH TO LOOSEN TEETH

Captain Alan Leahy CBE DSC

During my time in 803 Squadron our weapons were limited to 30mm cannon, 3-inch rockets (as used by the Swordfish in World War II) and 25-pound practice bombs. Ground targets on the firing range were used for cannon and bombs, but the rockets were generally used against splash targets towed by the ship. The cannon and rockets were quite spectacular against the splash target, and when firing all four cannon the noise and vibration were enough to loosen the pilot's teeth. The vibration was also sufficient to upset the serviceability of the Scimitar, so we tended to limit our practice firing to a pair of cannon. In addition to dive bombing with the 25-pound bombs, we practiced loft bombing or LABS, which was designed to allow the Scimitar to use the atom bomb.

When embarked we carried out a lot of combat air patrol sorties, or CAP sorties as they were known. The combination of HMS *Victorious*'s Type 984 radar and the Scimitar made, in our unbiased opinion, for the best day fighter system in the business. One exercise that was practised was to keep the CAP on the deck at alert. The pilot would man the aircraft, and after carrying out all his pre-take-off checks would sit back in the cockpit and wait to see if there was going to be any trade. Sometimes you could be sitting in the cockpit for so long that you would become convinced that nothing was going to happen on your stint when suddenly you would get the message to scramble. Both engines would be started at once, and before you could make sure that you had not forgotten anything you would be gone. It would have been better if we had had an air-to-air weapon to take with us, but that did not come until later.

In all I achieved just under 200 hours' flying time in the Scimitar, together with 100 deck landings—which included four night deck landings. My considered opinion, as a day fighter pilot, was and is that four night deck landings was four too many.

Apart from that, the rest was magic!

After the Scimitar was retired from service it was flown and maintained by Airwork Ltd and its role was as a target for ship's radars so they could be calibrated as the Scimitar cruised back and forth. No deck landings, no catapult launches, no high-'g' manœuvres, no 30mm cannon firing . . . and the serviceability was fantastic!

Below: Two Scimitars of 803 Squadron ready to scramble from the bow catapults of HMS *Victorious* in 1959. The catapult strops are in place and the aircraft are nose-high, their retractable tailskids touching the deck, in order to provide a high angle of attack and therefore maximum lift as they depart. The Type 984 radar referred to by Captain Leahy can just be seen in the top right-hand corner of the photograph, dominating the carrier's superstructure above the bridge.

SCIMITAR

Left: An 803 Squadron Scimitar, XE214, test-fires a Bullpup missile, 1962. Below: XD268, also of 803 Squadron, was used in trials of the Bullpup missile some two years earlier and was fitted with recording equipment beneath the starboard wing (visible in silhouette in this photograph). In 1959 this particular aircraft had triumphed in the *Daily Mail* London to Paris Blériot Anniversary Air Race, setting a time of 43 minutes 11 seconds. The pilot on that occasion was Commander I. H. F. Martin.

The Scimitar was also a very effective ground-attack aircraft, capable of carrying a variety of conventional ordnance. It could be armed with either 500lb or 1,000lb HE, SAP or AP bombs, one on each of the four wing pylons. Optionally, for training purposes, it could carry a maximum of eight 25lb practice bombs on the same stations.

The standard angle in a dive attack for Fleet Air Arm fighter-bombers was 20 degrees, which allowed pilots to operate in relatively low cloud bases of about 2,000 feet. In addition, this dive gave the shortest possible warning to the enemy of an attack and offered a safer pull-out height in order to avoid AA fire and bomb fragmentation damage. Target tracking was straightforward, and the aircraft remained steady in the dive and easy to correct.

The Scimitar was also well suited to high-speed, low-level bombing. The pilot flew as low as possible—50 to 100 feet above the sea on radio altimeter—and as the target passed under his nose he squeezed the bomb release trigger and made a sharp pull-up in order to avoid the resultant explosion and debris. I can remember once carrying out a low-level bombing demonstration off Malaya for the Prime Minister of that country, Tunku Abdul Rahman: apparently, I was so low that my jet efflux was creating a wash in the sea astern of the aircraft—which had Commander (Air) very worried (although I gather that the PM was impressed).

An alternative weapon for the air-to-ground role was the Bullpup, which was originally developed for the US Navy. The Scimitar could carry a maximum of four of these missiles. The Bullpup was an effective weapon, but aiming and steering it was far from easy, and called for considerable practice.

The problem was, for the most part, keeping the delivery aircraft in a steady dive with the gun sight aiming point also steady on the target while steering the missile. There was no real perception of depth and thus it was difficult to know exactly where the missile was in relation to the target during its flight, so it was incumbent upon the pilot to bring the missile to the aiming point as quickly as possible before it struck either the target or the ground. The

A DUBIOUS HONOUR
Commander Dave Howard

The Scimitar was the first 'heavyweight' aircraft I was to fly, and the first twin-engined type. It was a big, single-seat beast powered by two Rolls-Royce engines each producing about 10,000 pounds of thrust. On my first familiarisation sortie I lined up on the runway and settled back firmly in the ejection seat. I had been advised that the acceleration would surprise me, and it did. I really felt pushed back into the seat as I screamed down the runway, lifted off and climbed away. The speed build up was as nothing I'd ever experienced before and was really exhilarating. In no time at all I was shooting through 20,000 feet and on my way to 35,000 faster than I'd ever been.

And there the problems started. The Scimitar was not an aircraft for altitude. True, it could get up there really fast but, when there, its manœuvre capability was severely limited. Turning was almost a joke, the aircraft being 'on the burble' of the high-speed stall most of the time. The only thing to do was to ease the turn and wander round it slowly, as best you could. I only ever met one aircraft worse at altitude than the Scimitar and that was the US Navy's F3H Demon, an aircraft so poor at height that it became the subject of a Congressional inquiry.

But come down to low level in the Scimitar and then the fun really began. Here the aircraft was in its element—fast, fairly manœuvrable and very pleasant to handle. Its only problem down at that level was its fuel consumption. You could almost see the fuel gauges unwinding! Thumbing through my logbook I see that most of my Scimitar sorties occupied less than an hour, and on many of those longer than that I was able to in-flight refuel. Nevertheless, enjoy what you've got while it lasts, as they say—and I did. The Scimitar was a delightful aircraft to fly at the time I was flying it, although latterly it got terribly tired. It was only meant to be in service for four years as an interim aircraft between the Sea Hawk and the Buccaneer, but it eventually served for eleven. Some of the pilots in the final Scimitar squadron had had to eject more than once, the ageing aircraft they vacated having again developed another fatal fault that had made it imperative that they depart quickly.

Operating off the Philippines in 1962, I was given the dubious honour of trial-firing the first naval Bullpup missile. The Bullpup was a pilot-guided weapon that you fired in a shallow dive and then followed on behind, hopefully guiding it, by means of radio signals, on to the target. I think we had bought it cheaply from the Americans, who had quickly realised that what surface-to-air defences really like is an aircraft coming straight at them in a long, shallow dive: it gives them plenty of time to take aim and fire! Anyway, I hit the target (a rock), landed back on the carrier and was given another missile to fire for my next sortie. Good fun, yes, but of no operational use whatsoever!

800 Squadron had the lower hangar in 'Ark'. It was directly over the boiler rooms and, in the tropics, just one large sauna. To add to the discomfort for the maintenance crews, the Scimitar was a dirty aircraft. It had 'wet' wings—that is, fuel tanks in the wings themselves—and these seeped regularly. On top of this the aircraft leaked hydraulic fluid copiously. This meant that each aircraft had to have several large drip trays underneath it to catch this involuntary seepage and the maintenance crews were often sloshing around in the stuff. Thus maintaining the Scimitar, and getting sufficient numbers serviceable for the following day's flying, was an unpleasant task. Despite their awkward maintenance environment the crews always came up trumps for the following day's flying—helped by the fact that we didn't night-fly and the night maintenance watch at least had all their aircraft available to them.

Right: Lieutenant Dave Howard awaits launch on board *Ark Royal* in 1962, his aircraft armed with a pair of Bullpup air-to-ground missiles. Note the deeper pylon necessary for the missile compared to that required for the drop tank.

problem would eventually be overcome with the introduction of laser-guided weapons. The Bullpup's warhead was quite small in comparison with the size of the missile, but it could be effective against land targets; however, if fired against a warship the delivery aircraft stood a fair chance of being shot down.

Forward Air Control (FAC) was a system for ensuring that the delivery of conventional ordnance was as accurate as possible, and the Scimitar certainly played its part. Every British carrier had on board a FAC team, usually made up of an Army Captain or Major plus half a dozen NCOs and ORs, which could be 'choppered' ashore to a location

NUCLEAR SHAPES AND BULLPUPS

The Author

During my tour of duty with 800 Naval Air Squadron on board *Ark Royal*, I took part in a number of the dummy exercises that all carrier air crews conduct as a matter of routine. One such took place following a courtesy visit to Hong Kong while the ship was *en route* back to Singapore Dockyard for catapult and engine room repairs.

Being the Squadron's Air Warfare Instructor, I was one of four 'Strike Pilots' selected to carry out a dummy nuclear strike against a smoke float target with a 2,000lb 'shape'—i.e., a dummy nuclear bomb. A full briefing was carried out in the FAC Office, and the individual pilots were also briefed by the ship's Gunnery, Navigating and Met. Officers.

My Scimitar was launched over the South China Sea, my orders being to proceed south for about 300 miles, turn about and let down to sea level. Once at sea level I accelerated to 600 knots for the last fifty miles, flying over the smoke float and pulling up into a loop for an OTS (over-the-shoulder) weapon-release flying the LABS instrument in the cockpit. By keeping the cross-hair indicators in the middle I could fly a perfect 4g manœuvre. The smoke float had been placed equidistant between the carrier and its planeguard frigate. After I had turned through 90 degrees the weapon was released, and it continued vertically upwards to about 16,000 feet, whereupon it toppled over and headed seawards. I kept the aircraft in its loop, pulling hard down towards the horizon and diving away at full power and speed at sea level, placing my aircraft as far away as possible from the 'explosion'.

Following the sojourn at Singapore, *Ark Royal* sailed for East Africa and the Arabian Peninsula. En route selected Scimitar pilots carried out Bullpup air-to-ground missile firings against smoke targets in the middle of the Indian Ocean. The ship had on board the American Bullpup Trainer, which was set up in the FAC Training Office. Pilots would spend upwards of a couple of hours carrying out missile 'firings' against 'targets'. The task was not easy, and funnily enough the Squadron Line CPO was the best missile controller, playing it like a ping-pong machine!

Loading the Bullpup on to the aircraft was relatively straightforward. The ordnance groundcrew had a 'go'/ 'no go' piece of testing equipment. If the test equipment indicated the latter, the missile was simply unloaded, put back into its shipping box and returned to the manufacturer; no testing was carried out by the Ordnance Department on board the carrier.

A smoke float was laid by the ship's SAR helicopter and then a Scimitar would join the firing circuit, with a second aircraft circling overhead to plot the fall of shot and to ensure that the range was clear of any form of shipping. The firing pilot could make as many dummy dives as he wished, in order to fly the fighter accurately towards the target. One usually set the aircraft up at about 400 to 450 knots, set the throttle and trimmed the aircraft into a 20-degree dive, keeping the gyro gun sight's fixed cross on the target. There was always a tendency to accelerate down the dive and for the nose to come up with increased speed, but, finally, one found a comfortable speed and trim setting and a live run was made. There was not much time to gather the missile with its control stick in the cockpit and bring it on to the fixed cross and target before it impacted the sea. The weapon was ideal for firing from height and long range, thereby giving the pilot plenty of time to control it satisfactorily to impact, and most of us managed to achieve an impact within fifty yards of the target.

Left: Air brakes deployed for the dive, the author fires a Bullpup missile from the starboard outer pylon.

WEAPONS AND TACTICS

Above: An 803 Squadron Scimitar armed with four 1,000-pound bombs.
Below: 803 Squadron ashore at Lossiemouth. The aircraft nearest the camera can be seen to be carrying practice bombs on the outboard pylons.

close to the battle front line and therefore the enemy. The Scimitar pilot would approach the target area at about 250 feet AGL and 420 knots to pull up from an IP (Initial Point) and roll into a 20-degree dive over the FAC position at about 2,500 feet AGL. The FAC officer would then talk the pilot down to the target. If the attacking pilot was satisfied with his dive parameters and had the target in sight, he would release or fire his weapon(s). Depending on the result of the attack, the pilot would then either go around again for a furthert attack or be directed to another target—or, if all ordnance were expended, return to his carrier. This form of ground attack was one of the Scimitar's primary missions and it was practised frequently, especially off Aden and Malaya.

Each Scimitar squadron had a nucleus of aircrew designated the primary 'Strike Pilots', much of whose time was spent practising 'long toss' and 'over the shoulder' (OTS) nuclear weapon attacks using 258-pound practice bombs (which has ballistics similar to those of the 2,000-pound bomb). Each Strike Pilot would have a designated target that he would periodically study, the route to be followed, waypoints, target defences and other notable features of the mission also being scrutinised. Such a strike could be 'one-way' or 'there and back'—although of course it was fully realised that unforeseen circumstances could determine which in fact it would be. Usually once a year, a selected Strike Pilot would carry out a dummy mission. For this he would prepare his flight plan, which would be checked by the ship's Navigator, Gunnery Officer, FAC and Met Officer and the Squadron Air Warfare Instructor. His aircraft would be loaded with a dummy shape, he would man the aircraft and go through start-up in the hangar, and he would then be brought up to the flight deck, directed on to the appropriate catapult, and readied for launch. The pilot would carry out the sortie—of perhaps 300 nautical miles' range—and then return to make a low-level approach to release the 'weapon' against a smoke float. Back on board the carrier, he would taxi to a 'safe', isolated position on the flight deck, where the aircraft would be put through a 'decontamination' procedure; the pilot himself would himself be taken elsewhere to be 'decontaminated', which involved his stripping and showering and changing into clean clothing, his old flying kit being bagged up and destroyed. These days, of course, airborne nuclear weapons are not part of the Royal Navy's arsenal.

In 1964 800B Flight was commissioned, the CO being Lieutenant Roger Dimmock. He had command of four Scimitars which, fitted with three overload drop tanks and a refuelling pod, had been converted into in-flight refuelling tankers—in my view, much more effective in the role than their sister aircraft, the Sea Vixens. The Flight was based out of RNAS Lossiemouth, and embarked on board HMS *Eagle* with 800 (Buccaneer) Squadron as its support tanker element: when accompanied by a Scimitar tanker, a Buccaneer on a nuclear strike mission could reach many of its targets and return; the 'second leg' of this mission would otherwise would not have been possible. I recall carrying out a photo-recce flight from a launch position off Aden in my Buccaneer on one occasion, flying to the island of Socotra (a distance of 750 or so nautical miles from Aden), being topped up to the gills half way en route with 2–3,000 pounds from a Scimitar tanker of 800B, carrying out the mission at low level and then climbing out to altitude, coupling in the autopilot for a cruise-climb to 43,000 feet, and returning to the carrier. The total distance flown by the Buccaneer on this sortie was approximately 1,500 miles. On another occasion my Buccaneer was air-refuelled by a Scimitar over the south coast of France, having been launched off Algiers for a flight

Left: Scimitar tanker XD268, 800B Flight, releases its catapult strop as it roars off from HMS *Eagle*. 800B was the last front-line Scimitar unit to commission and the only one to operate from that carrier.

Below: XD244, a Scimitar of 803 Squadron, moments before launch from HMS *Victorious*, October 1961. Armed with a 2,000-pound 'shape', the aircraft is simulating the 'ultimate mission'.

back to RNAS Lossiemouth. I refuelled my aircraft to full capacity, slowly staggered to 35,000 feet and landed at Lossie with 2,000 pounds of fuel remaining, having flown a total distance of 1,300 miles.

Throughout the whole of its period of service, 800B Squadron did not suffer any incident or accident—a record that can be ascribed entirely to the taut reins on which Roger Dimmock kept his aircraft.

MAINTENANCE

THE Scimitar was equipped with two Rolls-Royce Avon turbojets each ultimately capable of producing 11,250 pounds (50.0kN) of thrust. The Avon was an axial-flow jet engine, but in this fighter it was not fitted with re-heat (afterburner) and therefore, except in a dive, the aircraft was incapable of supersonic flight.

The Avon owed much to the German BMW 0034-1 axial-flow turbojet engine built for the Heinkel He 162 and Junkers Jumo 004B designed and built for the Messerschmitt Me 262 twin-jet fighter, both of which appeared towards the end of World War II. It was an extremely powerful single-stage turbojet, and it and its derivatives powered a very wide range of aircraft types other than the Scimitar, for example the Sea Vixen, Lightning, Javelin, Hunter and Swift fighters and the Valiant bomber. The engine also formed the basis for the Roll-Royce Conway and the RB.200 series of bypass 'fan jet' engines, which consisted, in essence, of an Avon with a turbofan mounted at the front end, considerably increasing its thrust as a result.

The Avon would prove to be a very reliable engine for the Scimitar, and it was a great pity that it was not also fitted to the Buccaneer S. Mk 1 strike bomber instead of the De Havilland Gyron Junior. The main reason for that decision was that the Avon would have made the Buccaneer too heavy for the contemporary flight deck gear fitted on board Her Majesty's aircraft carriers, and it would be some time before the Buccaneer Mk 2 appeared with Rolls-Royce Spey bypass turbofans and flight-deck gear was upgraded in order to accommodate heavier aircraft.

The removal and servicing of the Scimitar's Avon engines was a relatively straightforward task, and the removal and replacement of one powerplant could be accomplished within a morning, ensuring that the aircraft was ready for test the same day following ground-running checks.

Generally, the Scimitar was an easy aircraft to maintain and most defects were either electrical or hydraulic in nature. One of the problems from which the aircraft suffered concerned its electrical fuel booster pumps. The fuel gauges were situated to the right of the main instrument panel, with the pump switches located beneath them. Initially, the first batch of aircraft had a limited number of booster pump switches, but subsequent batches of aircraft had a pump and switches for each fuel cell, thereby giving the pilot full control of his fuel load and the ability to select whatever tanks he wished. It was quite possible to fly the aircraft with all the booster pump switches selected 'off,' and thereby use gravity feed, but in this mode the pilot was restricted to gentle manœuvres. However, the aircraft suffered badly from fuel leaks.

Left: Routine checks for Scimitar XD322 on board *Ark Royal* in 1963, the 800 Squadron crest prominent on the aircraft's intake casing. Right: Lieutenant Phil Cardew and Pilot's Mate beautify their 803 Squadron Scimitar on board HMS *Hermes*, early 1963. Overleaf: A Scimitar under repair at Royal Naval Aircraft Yard Fleetlands, Gosport, winter 1959/60. Traces of 807 Squadron's scimitar emblem can just be made out on the fin of this aircraft.

THE NEED FOR DUSTBINS

Commander (AE) (P) Martyn Bolus

As the proud new AEO of 800 Squadron, I joined *Ark Royal* in Karachi late in 1963, and within a few days we were off to sea enjoying our standard 'twelve hours on, twelve hours off' in the discomfort of a very warm Lower Hangar. This was in the very early days of Tool Control—prototype wooden tool boxes—and during the second or third night that we were at sea my sleep was rudely disturbed when a hoarse voice said, 'You'd better come down to the Lower Hangar.' I staggered down there to discover that there was a very good reason for Tool Control, and I spent the next few days issuing amnesties for lost tools, as well as finding over a hundred missing items in some very strange places.

In my recollection, the worst thing about the Scimitar was its fuel system. Those who didn't know about it would listen with disbelief when told about the need for dustbins—lots of them—for any visiting Scimitar that was scheduled to reside in their hangar overnight. I think that the Scimitar was the first naval aircraft to have integral fuel tanks—in effect, just a sealant sloshed, carefully and scientifically, inside a large number of wing and fuselage compartments. This multiplicity of tanks was connected by a huge number of pipes and FR (flight refuelling) connectors, and, since this was in the days of area rule aerodynamics, the airframe designer had allowed a clearance of only about a quarter of an inch between these connectors and the airframe.

Fortunately in my time, we didn't have too many serious in-flight leaks, though I do remember seeing our 'on-loan' Frenchman downwind at Yeovilton streaming a large grey cloud behind him—no, not smoke, but fuel!—as a result of a major disconnection of a fuel pipe, which luckily hadn't happened whilst his section were providing air cover for the fleet out in the Atlantic!

And so back from *Ark Royal* to Lossie, where, thanks to a last-minute decision by FONFT staff, the Squadron were flown up to Scotland from Exeter in a very old, piston-engined Elizabethan, saving nearly two days of travel by British Railways. (The pilots flew off south of Plymouth and were home in fifty minutes!) The Scimitar was being phased out, and all thoughts—well, mine anyway—were on the Buccaneer and how we were going to make its automated weapons system work.

Thinking that the well-proven Scimitar was not likely to provide any new technical surprises, I was therefore startled one day to be told that four aircraft were returning to Lossie, led by the Boss, whose canopy had come off at altitude! A few minutes later a very windswept CO walked in. Investigation had shown that the mechanical hood lock could be dispensed with since the seal alone worked so well in keeping hood and aircraft together! Strange that this should not have happened before, given all the years that the Scimitar had been in service. And I can still remember the author flying the necessary pressurisation check after a new hood had been fitted, and writing an enormous '800' in the clear Saturday morning sky some 30,000 feet above Lossiemouth . . .

My time as a Scimitar 'plumber' was probably one of the shortest on record—just a few months at the end of 1963, after which 800 Squadron re-equipped with the Buccaneer. It was a relief to have new aircraft, even if they were Mark 1s. But I didn't get away with it completely, because 800 (Buccaneer) Squadron included four Scimitar flight refuellers—800B Flight—for whose maintenance I was also responsible. Luckily they were on the other side of the airfield, and their Chief AA was very good in not drawing too often on my limited experience. However, I did have one notable success, when the Flight had been quite unable to get the wings of one aircraft to spread: summoned across the airfield, and viewing the straining hydraulic test rig and the 24 or so sequence valves and locking jacks (rather like a nightmarish zip-fastener), I suggested 'helping' one of the valves with a screwdriver . . . and, suddenly, the wings miraculously spread!

ROYAL NAVY

XD267

FORTY-ONE

SCIMITAR

The two Avon engines rarely ever suffered from any in-flight defect and could be relied upon to perform regularly to specifications. On one occasion, while 800 Squadron was disembarked to Embakasi airfield at Nairobi, Kenya, the Squadron AEO had reason to change an engine because of damage to the turbine blades. The resident BOAC engineer officer happened to be visiting the Squadron at the time of the engine change and could not believe that the Navy would 'pull' an engine for what he termed 'minor damage': apparently, the BOAC Comet airliners' Avons would have had to have suffered far worse before *they* were 'pulled'! Throughout the the time that I flew the Scimitar, I was never aware of any pilot experiencing an engine failure or fire,

Above: XD222 under maintenance at RNAS Ford in 1958 in the early days of Scimitar flying. The aircraft is assigned to 700X Squadron, the Intensive Flying Trials Unit (IFTU).
Below: The Type 544 (N.113) WT854, the first prototype Scimitar, photographed at A&AEE Boscombe Down in early 1956. Note the stabilator dihedral—inverted for production aircraft—and the short dorsal intake fairing.

ated with the airspeed/height electrical system. When I was an

WALKING THROUGH SAWDUST
POEL(A) Bob Woods

I worked with the N.113s, on and off, from 1955 to 1958 at Boscombe Down. In my opinion, this aircraft represented the big turning point in terms of the maintenance of naval aircraft. It was the largest and heaviest aircraft we had met in our short naval careers. Fault-finding was unfortunately a frequent occurrence and in order to diagnose the problems properly one had to understand and work the large number of test sets that were at hand if required. At this stage of the Scimitar's test period most of the electrical gear was 'lifed', and fault-finding was sometimes down to black-box changing—a system that had its drawbacks as we rarely got to know the cause of a fault in the first place. Another strong memory is of leaks, drip-trays and dustbins in abundance, and of walking through sawdust to get near the aircraft (I exaggerate a little!).

Engine changes were at this stage something of a nightmare. For example, we had an N.113 arrive late one dark night, the test pilot indicating that it was due for a double engine change and that he was required to fly it the next day. This was to be our first N.113 challenge.

Work progressed through the night until it was time to replace the engines. The originals were removed, and the replacements were entombed in the bay from above, slowly lowering each one, with one electrician on top and one underneath, our job being to connect up the assorted harnesses. All was well until the second engine was installed and the associated bolts etc. were being put into place. It was then that one of the crew—in fact, the 'greenie' on top of the installed engines—indicated in a rather sickly voice that his foot had become, well, sort of 'jammed'.

This was not the most welcome news we wished to hear at that time in the morning: the crane had by this time gone and the thought of getting finished was at the forefront of our minds. Strangely enough, the Chief had by now turned a funny colour and all of a sudden had gone completely off 'greenies' . . .

The aircraft *did* fly on time, but during my time working with the aircraft I never once met a mechanic who loved a Scimitar.

neither did I hear of any such failures within the Fleet.

The aircraft did have a tendency to suffer from hydraulic failures when transiting from warm or hot climates to temperate or cold regions. This was brought about by the contraction or expansion of hydraulic pipe unions in sympathy with fluctuations in the ambient temperature and the leakages caused as a result. Oddly, *Ark Royal* herself used to suffer similar failures affecting her feedwater pump glands when moving from hot to cold climates, with the unfortunate result that the ship on occasion had insufficient feedwater to operate her engines and other equipment (including the steam catapults!).

Any electrical failures were usually associated with the airspeed/height electrical system. When I was an

SCIMITAR

instructor in 736 Squadron I repeatedly experienced an airspeed indicator failure with one particular Scimitar, and I eventually managed to persuade the Squadron Senior Pilot and AEO that the aircraft be grounded until a definite reason could be found for the failures. It finally transpired that the aircraft had some time beforehand ditched in the Persian Gulf, been recovered successfully, little damaged, and returned to the Naval Aircraft Repair Yard at Fleetlands, where it had supposedly been thoroughly

Below: Routine maintenance for 803 Squadron personnel topside on board HMS *Victorious* at Hong Kong, October 1961. In the foreground can be seen the port outer wing pylon and its (detached) wing fairing. Note the inevitable dustbins!
Above: Surplus to requirements: three Scimitars await disposal at RNAS Lee-on-Solent in the late 1960s following the type's withdrawal from service.. As is customary with 'tired' military aircraft, several Scimitars ended their useful days as static training specimens.

cleaned, overhauled and repaired. However, the cleaning process had not purged the airframe completely of its salt content, and it had to be withdrawn from service.

The Scimitar could sustain quite heavy damage and still continue to fly. For example, 800 Squadron while disembarked at RAF Tengah, Singapore, in 1963 had one of its aircraft severely damaged by a young pilot during an FAC training exercise. He had been flying over Jahore Barn to the north of Singapore, having been given a target by the FAC Army Captain, and he pulled out so low that he hit a ten-foot withey bush with his port drop tank. The bush was sliced in two, the drop tank front end shattered and damage was sustained by the port engine intake, leading-edge flap and undersurface of the port wing.

The young pilot then requested a re-strike, but the FAC officer—who by this time was on the verge of a heart attack—ordered him back to base. The pilot had no idea what damage his aircraft had sustained, neither had he any idea how close he had come to killing himself. On the way back to Tengah he did not experience any handling problems with the fighter, and it was only when he climbed out of the cockpit that he saw the damage that had been inflicted. The selfsame pilot had been involved in a similar incident over the FAC range north of Kuala Lumpur on the west coast of Malaya. Blades of grass were found in the perspex cover of the starboard wing-tip navigation light. He swore black was white that he had not been near the ground, and the FAC was unaware that he had made a low pull-out, so it must have happened either before reaching the range or after leaving it.

On another occasion an aircraft from 800 Squadron, flown by the late Commander Nigel Grier-Rees when he was a young Lieutenant, suffered a severe hydraulic failure over the Cairngorm Mountains in the north of Scotland and entered a steep dive. The pilot ejected with the jet then in a supersonic dive, and he suffered severe limb flailing which broke an arm and a leg. He landed in a deep snow drift and fortunately he was wearing an immersion suit, which protected him from the cold and from frostbite. Somehow he managed to crawl down the mountain and found a shepherd's bothy, where he spent the night. He was discovered the following morning. His aircraft had excavated a huge crater in the mountains and disintegrated.

Above: XD282 in 1962 at A&AEE Boscombe Down, in pristine condition following the repair necessitated by its brief flirtation with the Gulf of Aden (see page 27).
Below: A typical scene aboard HMS *Victorious* in the early 1960s as maintenance and flight-deck personnel go about their business. 803 Squadron's Scimitar XD234 is prominent, while Sea Venoms are parked on the port and starboard quarters of the flight deck and a pair of early-warning Skyraiders right aft.

OF MICRON FILTRATION AND DART TARGETS
Commander 'L. G.' Scovell

Joining the RN Test Squadron at A&AEE Boscombe Down in early 1957 as the Assistant AEO and Stores Officer was an exciting and challenging prospect for a young A/E specialist in his second appointment. The Controller of Aircraft (CA)'s Release Programme for the second generation of jet aircraft—Scimitar and Sea Vixen—and for the Seamew was in full swing, while the Buccaneer was also well advanced as a wooden mock-up at the Blackburn factory at Brough. Most of the aircrew were lieutenant-commanders, and all had qualified at the Empire Test Pilots' School; the Air Engineering Officer, Roger Heaton, was also a Maintenance Test Pilot. The Scimitar project pilots were Harry Julian (also A/E), Danny Norman and Sharky Robbins, and their patience, help and understanding were gratefully appreciated as I settled into an otherwise daunting situation.

The advanced hydraulic system of the Scimitar required a much higher standard of micron filtration than previous Royal Navy aircraft. However, the RN ground equipment inventory had not, unfortunately, kept pace with developments and no test rig was available. We therefore built our own—the 'Six-Five Special', named after a popular music programme on BBC television at the time. It may have looked Heath Robinsonesque, but it worked despite the difficulties of moving it about on detached trials.

Performance testing went reasonably well, but gun firing with the new Aden cannon caused an unexpected problem. The Scimitar had two triangular, titanium 'pen nib' fairings approximately three feet long, one on each side of the fuselage immediately behind the jetpipes. These were complicated fittings, curving in two planes. After a day's gun firing these fairings cracked and had to be welded overnight to meet the following day's schedule, but in 1957 titanium welding facilities were not available at all air stations, and Boscombe Down was one of these. The nearest facility for us was at the Supermarine works at South Marston, just outside Swindon, where an argon arc cabinet could handle one fairing at a time. It took almost an hour for the fairings to cool enough to be removed easily, so it was about three and a half hours after land-on that the fairings reached the facility. They arrived back at Boscombe Down at around six in the morning, allowing just enough time for them to be fitted for the first sortie of the day!

The targets towed by the ageing Gloster Meteors were not fast enough for Scimitar air-to-air firing exercises, so it was decided to use another Scimitar as the towing aircraft. How could this be achieved? An A-frame extension with a hook at the end was attached to the aircraft's existing deck hook frame, and a Dart target was laid out on the grass adjacent to the main runway with its towing rope flaked out ahead of it. At the head of the rope was a large loop draped over two 'goalposts' holding the top of the loop about ten feet above the ground. Originally, wartime Army Co-operation units had used this technique to pick up message containers with a Westland Lysander, the latter flying straight and level and probably at a speed of less than 80 knots—which was well below the stalling speed of a Scimitar. Moreover, at slow speed the attitude of the Scimitar was such that the pilot's eye level was many feet above that of the normally extended deck hook—and higher still above the hook extension.

The first attempt to pick up the rope was rather sporting! Sharky Robbins approached at 120 knots plus. The extension hook dug into the grass picking up a sod of earth so solid that the hook bumped over the loop but failed to pick it up. Needless to say, Sharky's subsequent attempts were slightly higher, and as a result the method proved to be successful and was adopted for shore use. It may have been used at sea with the rope flaked out ahead of the arrester wires on the carrier, but the towing aircraft had to land ashore as there was no way of jettisoning the hook extension.

A typical example of life on a test squadron when dealing with a prototype aircraft and support equipment (or lack of it) was out first double engine change—which had its moments of anxiety. As usual, the action was undertaken by the night watch. The first indication that all had not gone exactly to plan was the sight of our stalwart Chief Aircraft Artificer, CAA Potter: his hair was noticeably greyer than it had been the day before! On entering the hangar the aircraft was weighted down at the front with anything heavy that could be found, including an old railway sleeper. What oddments we had around us in those days! Apparently, as the lift of the second engine began the Scimitar started to tilt nose-up. Fortunately, when the engine was lowered back to its original position no damage had been sustained. As one would expect, a draft amendment to the Air Publications was in the post by lunchtime!

Right: First sea trials for the Scimitar's CofA Release Programme, HMS *Ark Royal*, July 1957. A Sea Vixen is being launched off the port catapult.

SCIMITAR

Above: Another retired Scimitar—and one that can still be seen today: this is the Fleet Air Arm Museum's XD317, shown here in July 1992 but these days under cover as part of the 'Carrier Experience' exhibit.
Left: The same aircraft in a earlier incarnation—at Hurn in June 1967 when being flown by Airwork (Fleet Requirements Unit) with a Harley light installed in the nose.
Below: Immaculate line-up of 803 Squadron Scimitars at Lossiemouth, armed for an practice sortie.

NOT EXACTLY TO PLAN

Commander 'L. G.' Scovell

I recall the occasion when a student Scimitar pilot on his first in-flight refuelling sortie disengaged so sharply that not only did his aircraft detach from the drogue as normal but the hose detached from the buddy pod as well. The now independently airborne hose and drogue wrapped itself around the student's aircraft caught between the refuelling probe and the nose, and the drogue had sufficient hose attached to flail between the windscreen—which it smashed—and the housed nose wheel door. The drogue was of a cast construction and shattered into pieces every time it struck the fuselage, and these metal fragments were of course immediately ingested by the two Avon engines along with the glass fragments from the broken windscreen! In the meantime, the rest of the hose deployed along the top of the Scimitar's fuselage stretched out in the airstream.

Despite the damage, the Scimitar and its 'attachments' could still fly and manœuvre, but the student could not see through the damaged windscreen against the considerable airflow. The instructor, Lieutenant 'Curly' Wood, flew alongside to confirm that there was no more obvious damage, declared an emergency and talked the student down on instruments and radio instructions in a 'parallel pair' landing. As the two aircraft touched down safely they were chased along the runway by the ever watchful fire crews—which was fortunate, because as the air speed decreased the end of the longer section of hose dropped from the top of the fuselage, spilling the residual fuel over the hot jet efflux The aircraft were stopped on the runway, the fire was extinguished and the remains of the hose and drogue were removed. The Scimitar required a double engine change and major airframe repairs to the engine intakes, the nose and cockpit glazing.

Both pilots received well-deserved Green Endorsements for their professional handling of a serious situation and safely recovering a damaged aircraft without further loss.

Above and left: The damage incurred by XD232/'611' of 736 Squadron on 5 June 1964 following an over-enthusiastic 'buddy-buddy' inflight-refuelling disengagement by the student pilot, as described by Commander Scovell in his article.

SHIPS AND SQUADRONS

THE Scimitar Intensive Flying Trials Unit (IFTU) was established at RNAS Ford (HMS *Peregrine*) in August 1957 as 700X Flight and remained in being until May 1958, exploring the capabilities of the aircraft and honing it into the optimum fighting machine that the Royal Navy required. Immediately following this the first front-line unit, 803 NAS, was established at RNAS Lossiemouth (HMS *Fulmar*), where, before the end of 1958, 807 NAS also re-formed, 803 meanwhile having embarked on HMS *Victorious*. The dedicated OFS2 (Operational Flying School Part 2), 736 NAS, was equipped with Scimitars by mid-1959 and it continued its role with the aircraft for a further six years until, in 1965, much of its task was transferred to the short-lived 764 Squadron. 800 Squadron re-formed with Scimitars on 1 July 1959 and the final full squadron, 804, re-formed on 1 March 1960. During its existence as a Scimitar unit 800 saw service aboard *Ark Royal*, 803 aboard *Victorious*, *Hermes* and *Ark Royal*, 804 aboard *Hermes* and 807 aboard *Victorious*, *Ark Royal* and *Centaur*. Scimitars also saw service on *Eagle*, 800B Flight serving as a tanker unit on board that carrier in 1964 and 1965.

There was a good deal of camaraderie within the ships' air groups, due in some considerable part to the fact that the Sea Vixen and Scimitar crews had initially all been trained together, until they separated at the end of OFS1, proceeding to Day Fighter OFS2 at Lossiemouth for Scimitar training or Night Fighter OFS2 at Yeovilton for Sea Vixen training. The Sea Vixen crews always thought

Opposite: HMS *Ark Royal* arriving at Hong Kong in 1962, manning ship and with six of her 800 NAS Scimitars ranged at the bows.
Above: HMS *Victorious* arrives at New York, 30 July 1959, her 803 Squadron Scimitars ranged amidships.
Below, Scimitars also served on HMS *Eagle*, 800B Flight—two of whose aircraft can be seen forward—serving in the tanker role, principally for the benefit of the short-legged Buccaneer strike bombers.

themselves a 'cut above' day fighter pilots as they had to fly at night and in all weathers. However, this really was not the case because the Scimitar, although not cleared for night deck landings except in an emergency, could fly in some of the most atrocious weather imaginable, the pilot relying upon his Direction Office in the ship's Operations Section to guide him. If the target were flying in cloud, then the Scimitar pilot did not have the benefit of the airborne radar fitted in the Sea Vixen (although he had a small radar ranging set in the aircraft's nose). Moreover, in many ways the Scimitar pilot had to be of a higher standard because he had only himself to rely upon, whereas the Sea Vixen pilot had his observer as well as his radar to assist him It is much the same these days in the RAF, where the Harrier pilots are considered by some to be the 'cream of the crop'.

The last but one front-line Scimitar squadron to be embarked was 800 NAS aboard *Ark Royal*, which disembarked to Lossiemouth on 30 December 1963. 803 Squadron disembarked and disbanded at Lossiemouth on 1 October 1966. 800 Squadron re-equipped with Buccaneer S. Mk 1s during March 1964. In fashion, 736 Scimitar Training Squadron was disbanded and resurrected a while later as the Buccaneer OFS2 Training Squadron.

SCIMITAR

800 NAVAL AIR SQUADRON

'Nunquam non Paratus'

Commission	Commanding Officer	Senior Pilot	AEO
01/07/59–00/02/64	Lt-Cdr D.P. Norman AFC	Lt N. J. P. Mills	Lt D. H. Pepper
		Lt-Cdr T. F. B. Young (03/08/60)	
		Lt-Cdr J. A. D. Ford (05/06/61)	
	Lt-Cdr A. J. Mancais (02/10/61)	Lt-Cdr D. F. Mills (17/12/62)	Lt-Cdr M. Scadding (27/04/62)
	Lt-Cdr P. G. Newman (25/03/63)	Lt J. D. H. B. Howard (00/00/63)	
	Lt-Cdr D. F. Mills (15/04/63)	Lt-Cdr J. F. Kennett (25/10/63)	Lt-Cdr M. H. Bolus (29/11/63)

Right: XD325 takes the wire aboard a rain-soaked flight deck, *Ark Royal*, 1963. A refuelling pod, its blades whirring, is carried on the starboard inner pylon and practice bomb racks are seen on the outer.

Above: Sub-Lieutenant Ian Frenz about to depart in XD280, *Ark Royal*, 1963. 800's squadron markings did not change throughout its existence as a Scimitar unit: red fin with 'R' for *Ark Royal* (the only carrier it embarked upon) plus call-signs boldly proclaimed on the nose in white-outlined black numerals.

Left: Ian Frenz poses with his Scimitar, XD322, while on detachment to Embakasi, Kenya, during the second half of October 1963.

FIFTY-TWO

SHIPS AND SQUADRONS

Above: XD272 *hors de combat* on board *Ark Royal* in 1963, securely lashed and with its vitals protected against damage following a problem with the aircraft fuel transfer system. The tail of a Sea Vixen from 890 NAS can be seen at left.

Below: A view aboard *Ark Royal* at the time of the author's service with 800 Squadron, the photograph taken in November 1963 during the occasion of a visit by personnel serving aboard USS *Essex*. The flight deck is a veritable hive of activity: together with two Scimitars of 800 NAS, five Sea Vixens of 890 NAS and a helicopter of the Ship's Flight (close to the round-down), two US Marine Corps A-4 Skyhawks are present and, aft, the Sea King that has brought visiting US Navy officers aboard.

FIFTY-THREE

SCIMITAR

Showtime! As the Royal Navy's premier fighter aircraft in the late 1950s and early 1960s, the Scimitar was frequently called upon to 'fly the flag' for the Fleet Air Arm, and all the principal squadrons equipped with the aircraft formed display teams at some point in their commissions.

This page, top: Formation practice close to the shore base, RNAS Lossiemouth, in 1961.
Above: Ready for Farnborough 1961, with the underwing serials suitably replaced. An Indian Navy Sea Hawk can be seen at left.
Opposite page: Displaying at the 1961 SBAC show at Farnborough, September 1961. Two of the aircraft retain their underwing serials.
Main image: 800 NAS at Le Bourget for the Paris Air Show, June 1961. The Squadron dubbed the team *The Red Blades* for the season.

FIFTY-FOUR

SHIPS AND SQUADRONS

FIFTY-FIVE

SCIMITAR

Above: The view from *Ark Royal*'s bridge of Lieutenant Walkinshaw's Scimitar following its brush with the starboard forward Bofors mounting—which appears to be relatively undamaged—as a result of brake failure while taxying, 30 May 1963.

Below: A successful arrest for XD322. late 1962 or early 1963. The ever-present rescue helicopter from the Ship's Flight can just be discerned behind the nose gear leg: in the event of a mishap, the pilot was assured of attention within minutes if not seconds.

THE MOST THRILLING OF AIRCRAFT

Lieutenant-Commander Bob Edward

800 Naval Air Squadron formed with Scimitars on 23 June 1959. The CO was Lieutenant-Commander Danny Norman AFC, the SP Lieutenant N. J. P. ('Freddy') Mills and the AEO Lieutenant Dave Pepper, the remaining pilots being Lieutenants Roy Noyes, Bill Thorpe and me, Flight Lieutenant Mumford and Sub-Lieutenant Bill Ryce. There were also a deputy Engineer Officer and a couple of Electrical Officers. We had six aircraft and shared a hangar—K 16, I believe—at RNAS Lossiemouth with 807 Squadron, who had eight Scimitars and whose CO was Keith Leppard. Both squadrons joined HMS *Ark Royal* in late February 1960; I left 800 at Malta on 12 May 1960.

800's primary role was nuclear (2,000lb bomb) strike, for which the aircraft were equipped with LABS (Low Altitude Bombing System); the secondary, and probably most important, role was ground attack and photographic recce and the tertiary role air defence. 807 had the same roles but in the reverse order.

There was no Scimitar simulator at that time. Briefing on the aircraft was given by the CO, who had flown the aircraft in his last job as SP RN Squadron Boscombe Down. I well remember my first familiarisation flight: line up on the runway . . . brakes on . . . up to 80 per cent on both engines . . . brakes off . . . increase to 100 per cent . . . fierce acceleration—so much so that I eased back on the power slightly!—ease back on the stick . . . nose up a bit . . . and airborne! Wheels up . . . and then I put all the power back on! What a wonderful sensation—the Scimitar was without doubt the most thrilling of aircraft.

On 20 January 1960 I went to HMS *Victorious* for two days' deck-landing practice and on 4 February to *Ark Royal* for wire-pulling trials and catapult shots following her refit. March saw us in the Med working up. We used the Tahuna range in North Africa for LABS training and the Malta Range (Filfla) for ground attack.

During my time in 800 the aircraft were not cleared for night deck operations, and in the early stages serviceability rates were bad: in eight months I only had 138 hours. However although the hours were few they were immensely pleasurable.

My second Scimitar tour was second-line training in 736 Squadron at Lossiemouth. The CO was Lieutenant-Commander Pete Newman, the SP Lieutenant-Commander John Kennett, the AWI myself, the QFI Pete De Souza, the Tactical Instructor Paddy Anderson and the Simulator Officer Maurice Hynett. I was there from 12 January to 20 December 1962. Our primary role was as Scimitar Operational Flying Training—providing conversion to the aircraft for pilots and maintainers—although we were given a secondary role of providing a display for the 1962 Farnborough air show . . . as described on page 83.

Left: 800 Squadron's Scimitar '103'—possibly XD239—in characteristic attitude on board HMS *Ark Royal*, circa 1962; an SAR Whirlwind helicopter hovers off the port bow. Quite what is taking place aft, engaging the attention of the flight-deck handling crews, is not known.

Right: The world's first supersonic beer? Squadron personnel pose with staff from Allsopp's (East Africa) Ltd at Embakasi to celebrate the carriage of a bottle of pilsner lager through the sound barrier by *Capitaine de Corvette* Michel Borney, an exchange pilot from the *Aéronavale*.

SCIMITAR

800B FLIGHT

Commission
00/09/64–00/08/66

Commanding Officer
Lt-Cdr R. C. Dimmock
Lt-Cdr N. Grier-Rees (20/10/65)

Senior Pilot
Lt I. P. F. Meiklejohn (02/12/64)

AEO
—

COURTESY REAR-ADMIRAL ROGER DIMMOCK

FIFTY-EIGHT

SHIPS AND SQUADRONS

Opposite: The Flight's commissioning ceremony at Lossiemouth, 9 September 1964.
Main image: Scimitars of 800B Flight, their tailfins displaying the famous frothing tankard insignia, on the line at RNAS Lossiemouth in September 1964. Late in their careers, Scimitar airframes featured additional cooling intakes, along the fuselage beneath the port wing root, between the cannon troughs on the starboard side and, as shown here, atop the rear engine casing, port and starboard. Communications aerials also changed through the aircraft's period of service, but apart from these minor 'upgrades' and the change in nose profile introduced very early on—and of course the addition, from *circa* mid 1961, of the inflight-refuelling probe—the external airframe was subjected to no significant modification.

FIFTY-NINE

SCIMITAR

Above: Steam rising from the slot, a Scimitar of 800B Flight is prepared for departure from *Eagle*'s waist catapult. The Flight's aircraft carried their call-signs mid-fuselage rather than on the nose.
Left: Personnel of the Flight photographed on board *Eagle* in 1965.

SHIPS AND SQUADRONS

Right: Squadron personnel pose with representatives of Whitbreads brewery, with which 800B had a close association—which in turn explains the fin emblem adopted by the Flight!

Below: Not quite what it seems: a Scimitar in flawless condition at Lee-on-Solent in July 1969. However, the tankard emblem is misleading since although this aircraft did indeed serve with 800B Flight, it saw out its service with 803 Squadron (hence the call-sign) and by the time this photograph was taken was being used for ground instruction.

Below: Another view of the Flight's aircraft at the time of its commissioning in 1964. The aircraft in the foreground has the 'photo-pack' nose cone: containing three F95 cameras, looking sideways and forward, this optional fit enabled the Scimitar to carry out basic photo-reconnaissance duties. A Hunter G.A. Mk 11 can be seen in the distance.

SIXTY-ONE

SCIMITAR

803 NAVAL AIR SQUADRON 'Cave Punctum'

Commission	Commanding Officer	Senior Pilot	AEO
03/06/58–00/10/66	Cdr J. D. Russell	Lt-Cdr G. R. Higgs	Lt-Cdr D. G. Titford
	Lt-Cdr G. R. Higgs (25/09/58)	Lt E. R. Anson (25/09/58)	
		Lt-Cdr P. S. Davis DSC (24/09/59)	
	Lt-Cdr A. J. Leahy MBE DSC (14/12/59)	Lt-Cdr C. S. Casperd (10/11/60)	
	Lt-Cdr T. C. S. Leece (18/12/60)		Lt E. O. Tonkin (12/12/61)
	Lt-Cdr N. J. P. Mills (01/08/62)	Lt-Cdr G. A. I. Johnston (16/12/63)	Lt-Cdr (E) (M) A. Reynolds (13/06/63)
		Lt G. H. J. Daykin (06/01/64)	
	Lt-Cdr P. G. Newman (04/05/64)	Lt-Cdr J. W. H. Purvis (22/05/65) (14/12/64)	Lt-Cdr (E) (M) A. Wormell
	Lt-Cdr J. Worth (14/06/65)		

Main image: HMS *Victorious* in 1959, with five Scimitars of 803 Squadron on the flight deck, together with Sea Venoms and a lone Skyraider.
Left: XD331 seconds from launch, HMS *Victorious*, 1960.

LOADED WITH TALENT

'A Squadron Officer'

My overall recollection of my time on 803 was that it was a fun squadron, particularly after 'Spiv' Leahy joined as CO—and life was never dull with the likes of John Beard and Fred de Labilliere around. We had some very talented pilots: I believe we had five ETPs (Empire Test Pilots) in the Squadron when I joined. The FAA were worried about whether pilots could cope with the nose-up landing attitude of the Scimitar on approach to the deck, and had, therefore, loaded the IFTU with talent, which was still there when we became 803.

I recall taking a Scimitar to the butts at Lossie one day to harmonise the Adens, and to check where the shells were actually going. No pilots were available so I decided in the end to fire them myself! One of the mainwheel lashings broke, causing the aircraft to yaw as it was thrown backwards by the recoil of the four cannon, and I sprayed quite a wide arc of Speyside with 30mm at 400 rounds a minute before releasing the firing button. As fortunately no one was hit, we managed to keep things quiet, but I got a good scolding from Ollie Greenhalgh.

My other vivid recollection of these aircraft was of getting the engines to start on the catapult in damp weather. To assist them to start we used manually to lift the 'bobweight' on the fuel throttle in order to 'overfuel' the engine. However, if this was overdone it was a quick means of blowing up the engine, so the malpractice was restricted to the AEOs. Reaching the bobweight on the port engine necessitated inserting one's entire arm into a small door very close to the jet pipe, and the bang on light up was deafening. This practice was also very colourful at night, especially if the JBD (jet blast deflector) had not been raised in time. The resultant sheet of flame would reach the rear of the island. One did not stand behind a Scimitar on start-up!

'HERE'S A TRIDENT...'

Lieutenant-Commander Colin Casperd

My first stay with 803 Squadron unfortunately lasted only a fortnight as I was involved in a gliding accident and sustained an infected compound fracture of the right leg, resulting in a three-month sojourn in Elgin Hospital. However, the upshot was that although my leg was confined in a full-length plaster for almost a year I was at the time the only QFI who had flown Scimitars and by now there was a small trickle of candidates from basic flying training. I was therefore 'loaned' by the Sick Bay to 807 Squadron—by this time resident at Lossiemouth—to assist with their acquaintance course and familiarisation flights. It was chiefly classroom work using basic aids (it was, I think, early 1961 before a simulator was available), but I was also able—just—to clamber up the side of the cockpit to confirm the students' checks and see them off, followed by a dash to Air Traffic Control and another clamber up a vertical ladder to Air Watch in order to supervise the circuits. Health & Safety probably insist on a lift to Air Watch nowadays.

After a successful bone graft and rehabilitation, and then a short spell on Vampires and Hunters, I returned to 807 for full flying duties. The Scimitar's serviceability appeared to be good as I was carrying out three or four sorties a day and was soon back in the swing of things. Unfortunately my stay with 807 lasted only three months and I found myself in 764 Squadron and Hunter trainers, although this was also short-term: ten months later I was refreshing on Scimitars and off to Malta to re-join 803 in HMS *Victorious* as their Senior Pilot.

When I re-joined 803 most of the original pilots had left and the CO, 'Spiv' Leahy, was about to leave. However, I knew both the leaving and the joining COs: we had all been instructors in a Sea Hawk squadron and had also flown together in the Sea Hawk aerobatic team at Farnborough. The next twenty months, under Tom Leece, passed very pleasantly, with all the usual tasks and exercises that front-line squadrons perform during the course of a world-wide cruise. Initially we returned from Malta to spend Christmas at home but then it was off again to the Far East, taking in, *en route*, 'shop window' exercises off Cape Town and diverting to Kuwait as problems developed in Iraq. There were few lengthy rest periods ashore: most of the time it was hard work at sea, especially for the maintainers, who were working in tropical temperatures and humidity in a non-air-conditioned ship. Although our servicing crews did very well, we would have liked a few more flying hours, which were rationed so that the junior pilots had just about all they wanted and the senior pilots (CO, SP, AWI) made do with what was left over. Nevertheless, we all kept in good practice, with the specialist pilots (LABS, PR) maintaining their skills. We did, of course, have a few problems—and at least two tragedies. A hydraulic problem necessitated a planned ejection alongside the ship but, unfortunately, the parachute malfunctioned and the pilot was killed. On the other occasion, although the ejection sequence worked correctly, the pilot's legs 'flailed' in the descent and although recovered by helicopter he suffered internal injuries and died a few days later in hospital.

I was much more fortunate, completing a full tour with only minor mishaps that were more humorous than worrying, two occurring at night. On one occasion my cockpit lighting failed. The one important instrument for landing is the ASI, and at altitude, at dusk, there is sufficient light to enable the pilot to make sense of the instruments, but on descent the conditions change and it becomes much darker.

Below: Lieutenant Colin Casperd split seconds after making a touch-down on board *Victorious*, the rapid deceleration of the aircraft throwing him forward against the seat straps in the cockpit.

Above: 803 Squadron awaits the arrival of its Senior Pilot, May 1962.

Most of us carried a basic flashlight on a piece of string around our necks for emergencies and generally looking around the aircraft, but this night it became very useful for speed reading. One would always appreciate a third hand, so I duly lowered the oxygen mask and held the torch in my mouth. All right so far, but radio calls are necessary, and it is surprising how often you want to swallow. I still have that torch.

On another occasion I had been on a distant dusk LABS exercise and returned to find *Victorious* going round in circles, her rudder jammed. Fortunately *Ark Royal* was available and not a great distance away, but I knew that she had a different type of landing aid—one that I had not used, and certainly not at night! However, for a deck landing all you really require is air speed, centreline and angle of descent, and at night their sight gave exactly the same information as that in *Victorious*. I was well received by 800 Squadron, our chummy Scimitar unit, but in the morning, when I came to return to *Victorious*, I saw that my aircraft had been well and truly covered with messages. 800's emblem is a trident and ours a bee, and amongst the scrawl was the following gem: 'Cave Punctum / What a farce / Here's a trident / Up your ——'.

803 Squadron had departed from Britain a day fighter outfit but as the months progressed we became more and more involved with bombing, rocketing and LABS, so that by the time we returned home we were a strike squadron. Our Far East cruise ended in the Mediterranean, and we all flew home to Lossiemouth via Gibraltar to receive the standard welcome on the tarmac that squadrons have enjoyed for many years. I remained with 803 until May 1962, when I handed over to my great pal Brian Willson.

I was under the impression that I had had my last ride in the big beast, but this was not so. Two appointments later, I was on the Admiral's Staff at RNAS Yeovilton, a non-flying job although most of us flew whatever we could get our hands on in Station Flight so that we could visit all the air stations under the Admiral's command. Although Yeovilton was at this time a night fighter base with Sea Vixens, I am unable to recall anyone borrowing a Vixen: the Flight had a Swordfish, Tiger Moth, Vampire, Hunter, etc., but possibly not a Vixen. However, one day a Scimitar appeared at Yeovilton. I have no idea how or why. Had the pilot gone sick? Had the aircraft had a recent defect that had now been rectified? Whatever the reason, the problem was the Admiral's, and, of course, it soon became mine: it had to be returned to Lossiemouth. Although it was by now two and a half years since I had flown a Scimitar, it was absolutely no worry at all! I returned in a Hunter, which took a little longer.

So ended my six and a half years with the Scimitar—albeit not continuous. I enjoyed every minute of it. Depending upon one's background, the aircraft could be a handful initially, but after the first few sorties I felt perfectly at home.

Would I do it all again? Of course I would!

Below: Lieutenants Casperd and Willson inspect a Scimitar for FOD.

SCIMITAR

Above: A planeguard's view of an 803 Squadron Scimitar landing aboard *Victorious*, 1961.
Left, upper: 803 Squadron personnel in a photograph believed to have been taken in October 1961 while *Victorious* was visiting Hong Kong.
Left, lower: In 1962 HMS *Hermes* became 'home' for 803 Squadron, and at the same time the unit markings were changed. Initially a large letter 'H', raked backwards in conformity with the angle of the tailfin was adopted, as seen in this photograph of XD215 taken following a landing mishap in July that year. The change in fin *décor* was accompanied by a change in position of the aircraft callsigns.
Right, upper: However, the new marking quickly gave way to black and yellow checks, as seen here in 1963. This particular aircraft, XD333, was the very last production Scimitar.
Right, lower: With the Squadron's embarkation on *Ark Royal* in late 1964, the fin code letter changed appropriately.

SIXTY-SIX

SIXTY-SEVEN

SCIMITAR

804 NAVAL AIR SQUADRON

'Swift to Kill'

Commission
01/03/60–15/09/61

Commanding Officer
Lt-Cdr T. V. G. Binney

Senior Pilot
Lt-Cdr B. G. Young

AEO
Lt-Cdr (E) R. Baker

Above: A pair of Scimitars from 804 Squadron bank over the sea, their undersurfaces strongly highlighted. 804 was the shortest-lived of the four front-line Scimitar squadrons, its commission lasting just over eighteen months.

Above: XD326 on approach. Two Chief Petty Officers with the name 'Arnold' were responsible for the maintenance of this particular aircraft—hence the stylised 'Arnold Airways' legend on the intake casing, accompanied by the names of other ground crewmen.

Right: XD323 and XD325 over the North Sea up from Lossiemouth, the vacant practice bomb racks suggesting that the aircraft are on the homeward leg of an armament exercise. Three of the 200-gallon underwing tanks seen here have the front tips painted red.

SHIPS AND SQUADRONS

Above: HMS *Hermes* arriving at Gibraltar in mid-April 1961 with four 804 Squadron Scimitars topside amidships.
Left: 804 Squadron personnel in a formal photograph, 12 March 1961. XD326 in the background shows changes in 'ownership' compared with the photograph opposite.
Below: Navy Day, Portsmouth, 1961: XD274 in characteristic take-off attitude aboard HMS *Hermes*. Note the high-gloss finish of the paintwork: the Squadron emblem is sharply reflected in the tailplane.

SIXTY-NINE

WAS I INTERESTED?

Commander Giles Binney OBE

Sitting at my DNAW desk, supposedly dealing with the Scimitar but actually bemused and confused by the whole business of how the Admiralty worked, and with the awful prospect of another year to come, I was about to depart for Christmas leave 1959 when the phone rang. It was my friendly Appointer, Boot Nethersole. They needed someone to take the next Scimitar squadron, 804, forming at Lossie in three months' time. Was I interested? I would need to leave almost at once to get up there, do a bit of rehabilitation and then the Squadron CO's course. I could hardly believe that life could offer such a plethora of delights on a cold, dank, winter Whitehall morning.

804 was to be a small squadron—six to eight aircraft, depending on what was going on—destined for *Hermes* and together with 892 Vixens to form her first air group. Forming up in March, we would be embarking for work-up in July. It all seemed quite a rush. The first decision was whom to invite to commission us. It was usual to ask one of the air admirals (FONFT, FO Air, etc.), but I could see no advantage in this—they would be all too present in no time—and I decided to ask the local laird and distinguished Admiral, Sir Martin Dunbar-Nasmith VC. He had something none of the others had—excellent shooting and fishing—and he took to us with delight and we to him: he was a most remarkable and charming man. It seemed to me a slight downer that with the commissioning due in the afternoon none of us had actually flown the thing, so I managed to get our one serviceable Scimitar out of the hangar and, with much trepidation, into the air. It was a new aircraft and so relatively smooth, but the experience was memorable and during the march-past two hours later my sword arm was still shaking from the shock, 'buzz' and enormous fun of flying and barely controlling a 1,000cc motorbike with wings and a host of flashing lights all trying to tell me something.

During the four-month work-up period we were lucky with the weather and with excellent serviceability made good use of the ranges, including an exhilarating period down at West Freugh releasing 'shapes' (dummy nuclear weapons) in lobbing and 'over-the-shoulder' manœuvres. It was amazing to act as escort to a lobbing aircraft and follow his 'bomb' the five or six miles to the target. My own drops were mostly forgettable, but I well remember, with a degree of jealousy, David Mears getting it right every time (and, as Air Warfare Instructor, so he should have!). These LABS systems were the best available to us, and we took the role very seriously but without much optimism over the results.

By the time we formed up much had already been learned about the Scimitar, and we had the great advantage of the knowledge and experience gained (often at considerable cost) by Boscombe Down and the squadrons already formed and operating, so there were really no surprises and we were grateful for this. I am sure that there are contributions in this book from others far better qualified than I covering the performance aspects of the aircraft: things are always easier when others have paved the way, and none of us had any serious problems in mastering the aircraft and trying to get the best from it. Operating from the deck was no problem, but, like others, we were often handicapped, especially in the Far East, by lack of wind and of ship speed, resulting in those frustrating chases after apparent wind lanes, usually in the opposite direction to that in which we wanted to go.

The work-up in the Moray Firth went okay, though there was a slight personal embarrassment when my first landing on *Hermes* came only after four failed attempts and when on the verge of being sent back to Lossie—a fate that befell none of the others. I was lucky in many respects, in the ship with her superb Captain, David Tibbitts, and 'Wings' Ian Campbell, and most of all in the Squadron itself—Brian Young the Senior Pilot, David Mears our AWI, the aircrew and technical officers without exception, and the splendid Chiefs, POs and junior rates who kept us in the air, who worked frequently round the clock with good humour and who never caused me to doubt that an aircraft presented, often after an full night of work, was serviceable and safe to fly.

We sailed in *Hermes* in early July for the Med, returning to home waters in September. Then it was back to Lossie until November, when we made the interesting flight to Gibraltar/North Front to re-join *Hermes*. Radio/tacan links in France and Spain were supposed to help us on our way, but it must have been siesta time. Then it was out to the Far East and disembarkation to Kai Tak, where Jack Smith and Maurice Hynett excelled themselves by sonic-booming Kowloon, the 'lens' effect of the surrounding hills producing an interesting damage pattern. Next day the front page showed a victim, being shaved at the time, running out of the barber's with blood streaming down his neck. Windows and tiles were shattered over a large area, and I was pursued by legal writs around the Pacific.

Left: Officers of 804 Squadron: (left to right) Sub-Lieutenant (E) L. Carter, Sub-Lieutenant A. J. Gerry, Lieutenant-Commander (L) Charles Jackson, Lieutenant-Commander Brian Young (SP), Lieutenant John Faulkner, Lieutenant-Commander Giles Binney (CO), Sub-Lieutenant Jack Smith, Lieutenant David Mears, Sub-Lieutenant A. J. Stone, Flight Lieutenant Mike Webb RAF and Lieutenant Maurice Hynett.

Throughout 804's time embarked we were involved in the usual series of exercises and evolutions. At the time it all seemed pretty routine, but it has only been subsequently (and especially now, very much later) that I find myself looking back on those wonderful times as the best of my professional life. Philosophers are right in maintaining that we are often quite unaware at the time of being truly happy. After eighteen months in commission it was a great pleasure to me that we decommissioned without the loss of any of our aircrew or aircraft. I think we did quite well, and I cannot resist the temptation to quote one of Flag Officer Aircraft Carrier's readiness reports for March 1961: 'Scimitars 804 and 807 are congratulated on their returns . . . 804 achieved highest Scimitar readiness on record.'

We had our share of luck, some incidents being particularly memorable. Towards the end of the commission we were putting in a 'mini' performance at the Farnborough Air Show, the idea being to launch in the Channel, overfly Farnborough and return to the ship—a formation of ten Vixens and six Scimitars. Timing of course had to be precise, and our last checkpoint was to be Lasham. As we approached at 1,000ft and 350 knots, Lasham appeared on the dot, but—horrors!—the whole area was swarming with gliders. They had not been told to expect us! There was nothing we could do but plough on—which we did, to the accompaniment of what was described by those who witnessed it as the most remarkable mass glider evasion display imaginable. Would we perhaps like to try it again?

Next, an event that still gives me occasional nightmares. Hermes was to take part in a series of 'shop windows'—the sort of thing that all naval aviators know well. 804's centrepiece consisted of a dive-bombing attack by four aircraft, each carrying four VT-fused 1,000-pound bombs on a helicopter-dropped smoke float just over a mile on the port bow. This had gone very well in rehearsal, but on the day the smoke float failed to materialise and I was told by FLYCO to 'just drop them well away.' I thought I had, but on pulling round with the familiar backward look over the shoulder I was horrified to see the most awful sight down below. HMS Hermes, with the frigate HMS Puma about a cable on the starboard bow, was just approaching the froth and foam left behind by our sixteen 1,000-pounders and I could tell by a series of somewhat abrupt messages that the exercise had not gone down very well. Indeed, not only was Hermes packed with Staff College observers, etc., but, worse, the upper deck of Puma was covered in Sea Cadets. Nobody was hurt, but the Captain of Puma later sent on board two large sacks of splinters dug out of his ship, including a nasty thing about 18 inches long which had skewered the funnel. Hermes herself was also hit by a number of splinters. Captain David Tibbits' reaction was superb. He said, 'What you want to do is to get ashore and call on the Captain of Puma before he calls on me, You might even get a gin.' Commander Air, Ian Campbell, chimed in with, 'Do drop them a bit farther away tomorrow!'

Another memorable occasion was when on passage towards the western Med, preparing to take part in one of the periodic Kuwait/Iraq confrontations. FOAC, Admiral Dick Smeeton (an ex 804 man, incidentally), came down to the wardroom for dinner. Afterwards he challenged the squadrons to his favourite game, which involved lying on the deck 'fishing' for one's opponent's legs and upending them. There were no immediate volunteers, so he looked at me with that unique, challenging stare and I had no choice but to submit. It was all over in ten seconds and I was carried in acute discomfort and laid out on a sofa to the Admiral's amused disdain. He then went through all the 804 and 892 aircrew in quick succession, leaving us physically and mentally shattered, but the real problem surfaced next morning when we were all completely seized up and hardly able to move. The Captain then had the tricky task of informing the Admiral that, due to his personal actions, not a single member of the two squadrons was fit to fly. The Kuwait scare died down—which was just as well.

So after eighteen months ashore at Lossie and embarked it was all over, and after the last of our Farnborough appearances we returned to Lossiemouth to decommission and be greeted by the Captain, George Baldwin, with a signal just received from Hermes: 'Flying completed, and we send 804 Squadron back to you with regret after a splendid commission in Hermes.'

Right: HMS Hermes at Messina in July 1960 during the carrier's Mediterranean cruise. Two of 804's Scimitars are ranged on deck, together with four Sea Vixens and a pair of AEW Gannets. Note the ships's massive Type 984 (combined warning and interception) radar, a feature also of Victorious and Eagle (but not Ark Royal).

SCIMITAR

807 NAVAL AIR SQUADRON *'Quoquo versus Ferituri'*

Commission	Commanding Officer	Senior Pilot	AEO
01/10/58–15/05/62	Lt-Cdr K. A. Leppard	Lt-Cdr T. C. S. Leece	Lt-Cdr J. T. Checketts
	Lt-Cdr W. A. Tofts (01/10/59)	Lt F. Hefford (03/11/59)	Lt P. J. Flynn (22/06/60)
	Lt-Cdr G. A. Rowan-Thomson (01/03/61)	Lt J. W. Moore (26/06/61)	Lt-Cdr D. A. Vaughan (23/11/61)

Above: The 807 Squadron recommissioning photograph, 15 October 1959. The scimitar emblem selected for the fin *décor* was unrelated to the Squadron crest (which features seven daggers).

Below: Five of the Squadron's aircraft on parade at Lossiemouth at the time of recommissioning. All but '190' (XD243) have the last numeral of the call-sign repeated on the forward nosewheel door.

Right: The Squadron's first embarkation was aboard HMS *Ark Royal* but from April 1961 it was assigned to the light fleet carrier HMS *Centaur*. The tail code changed appropriately, and the call-sign on the nose now appeared in black with a white outline instead of gold with a black outline. This is XD216 at Lossiemouth.

SHIPS AND SQUADRONS

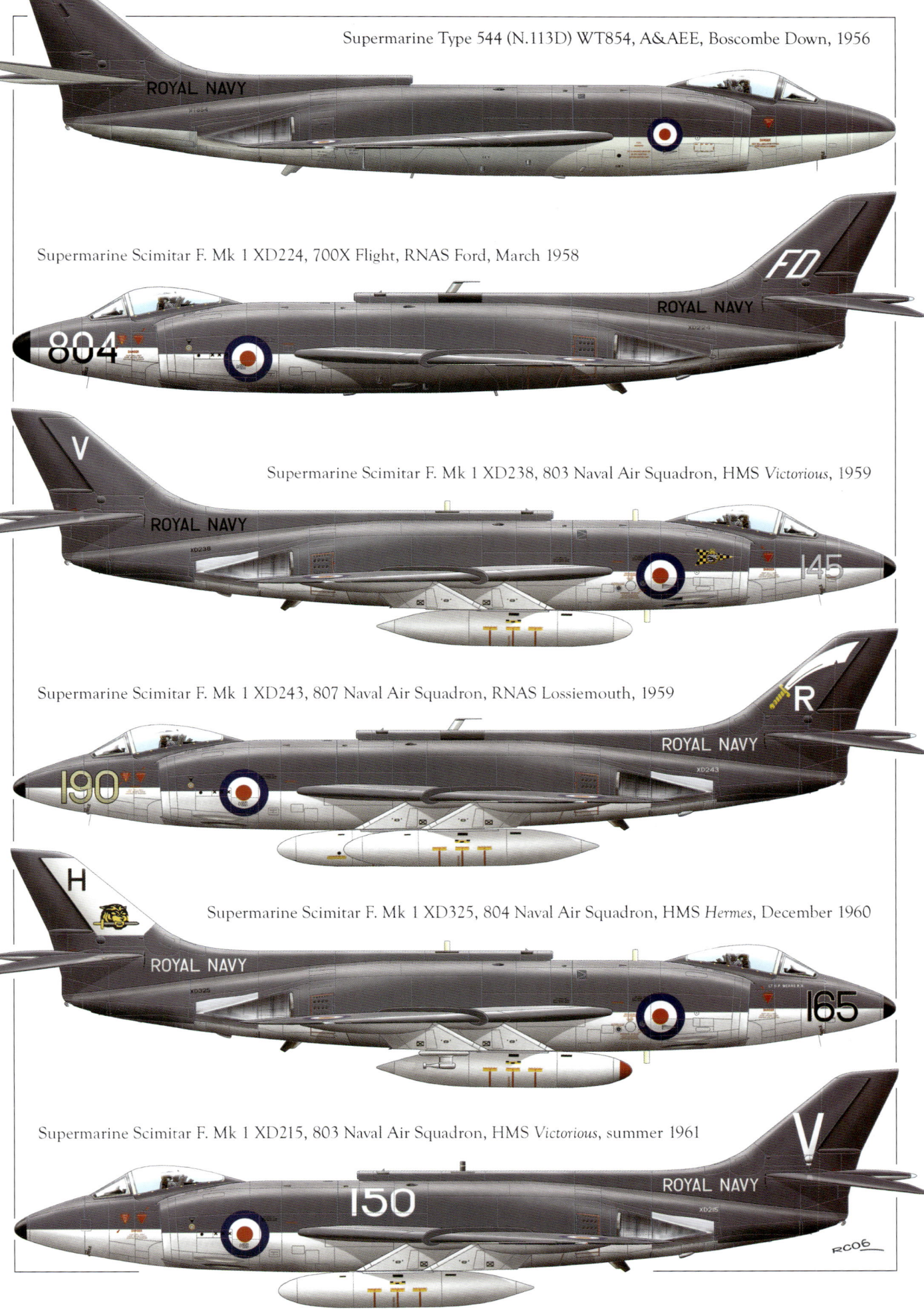

Supermarine Type 544 (N.113D) WT854, A&AEE, Boscombe Down, 1956

Supermarine Scimitar F. Mk 1 XD224, 700X Flight, RNAS Ford, March 1958

Supermarine Scimitar F. Mk 1 XD238, 803 Naval Air Squadron, HMS *Victorious*, 1959

Supermarine Scimitar F. Mk 1 XD243, 807 Naval Air Squadron, RNAS Lossiemouth, 1959

Supermarine Scimitar F. Mk 1 XD325, 804 Naval Air Squadron, HMS *Hermes*, December 1960

Supermarine Scimitar F. Mk 1 XD215, 803 Naval Air Squadron, HMS *Victorious*, summer 1961

SEVENTY-THREE

FLOWN BY THE AUTHOR

SUPERMARINE SCIMITAR F. Mk 1
XD321, 800 Naval Air Squadron, HMS *Ark Royal*, November 1963

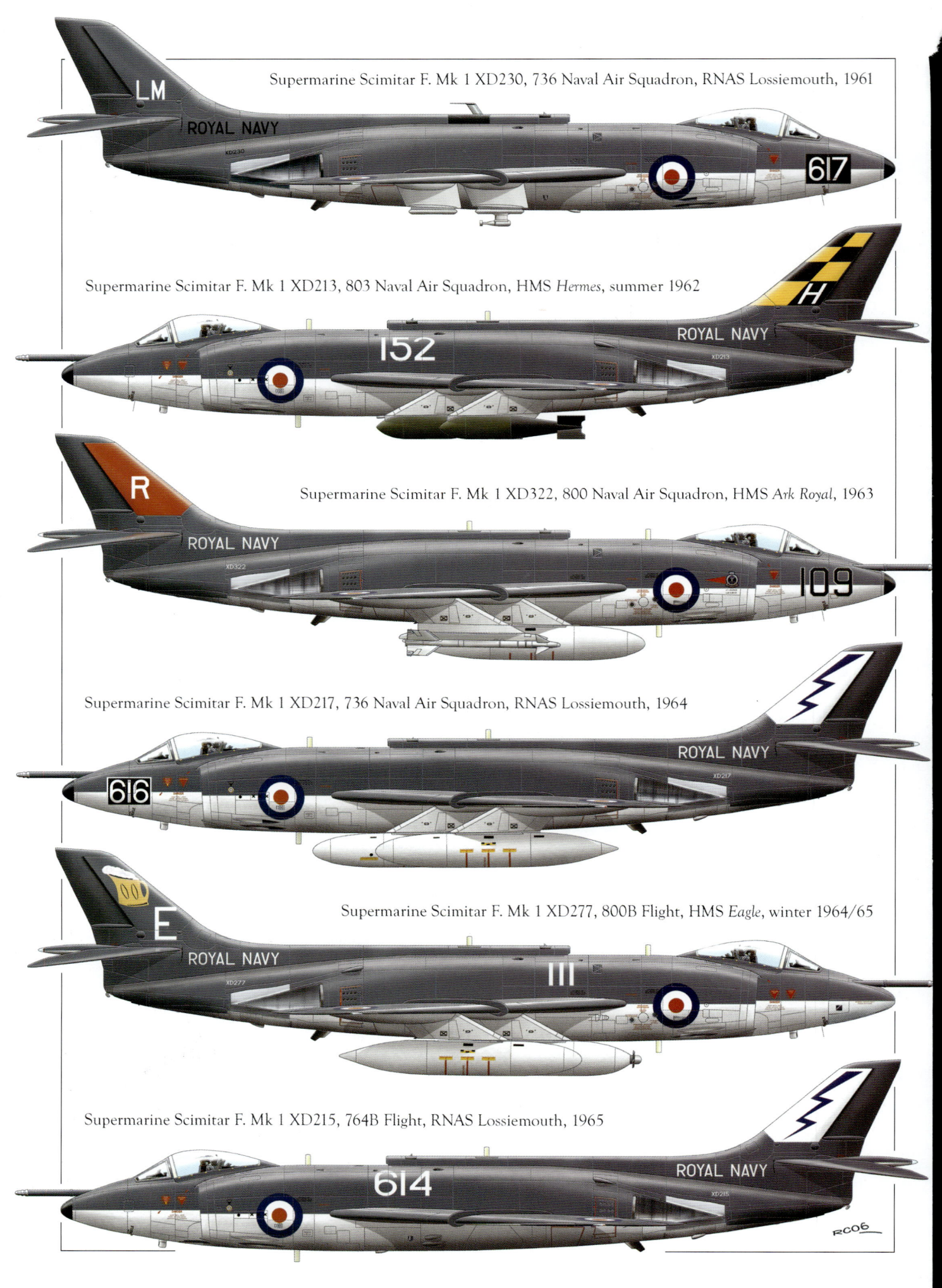

Supermarine Scimitar F. Mk 1 XD230, 736 Naval Air Squadron, RNAS Lossiemouth, 1961

Supermarine Scimitar F. Mk 1 XD213, 803 Naval Air Squadron, HMS *Hermes*, summer 1962

Supermarine Scimitar F. Mk 1 XD322, 800 Naval Air Squadron, HMS *Ark Royal*, 1963

Supermarine Scimitar F. Mk 1 XD217, 736 Naval Air Squadron, RNAS Lossiemouth, 1964

Supermarine Scimitar F. Mk 1 XD277, 800B Flight, HMS *Eagle*, winter 1964/65

Supermarine Scimitar F. Mk 1 XD215, 764B Flight, RNAS Lossiemouth, 1965

A PILOT'S AIRCRAFT

Captain K. A. Leppard CBE

Above: Four Scimitars from 807 Squadron, led by the CO, Lieutenant-Commander Keith Leppard, loop in box formation over the coast of the Moray Firth, 1959.

The powerful acceleration from two Rolls-Royce Avon engines giving 22,500 pounds of thrust on take-off and, as I recall, a spectacular climb to 30,000 feet in 3 minutes 50 seconds are the lasting impressions of my first flight in a Scimitar. It was a rugged and versatile aircraft of particularly strong construction and with an exceptional rate of roll at lower levels. As a ground attack weapons platform it was stable and flexible in its modes of delivery. Apart from 30mm cannon, rocket and bombing practice, 807 Squadron Scimitars were required to train in the Low Altitude Bombing System, colloquially known as the 'over-the-shoulder' method of delivering a tactical nuclear weapon. Traversing the Moray Firth coastline and hinterland at 50 feet and 540 knots was an exciting pastime! An extension of the deck arrester hook enabled high-altitude Dart targets for cannon-firing practice to be picked up in flight from ground rigs. Single-engine performance was excellent, as I experienced when a ricochet from my own cannon fire stopped the port engine dead during strafing practice. Safe recovery to RNAS Lossiemouth on one engine was straightforward and comfortable.

The culmination of my command time was as leader of 807 Squadron nominated as the Royal Navy display team at the 1959 Farnborough Air Show. Many of the Scimitar's impressive characteristics were demonstrated, including the innovative 'twinkle roll' of a 'Box Four' formation evolved by the Squadron and believed to be performed for the first time in public. This manoeuvre was subsequently adopted by many internationally known aerobatic teams. To conclude the show, an imaginary A-bomb was 'lobbed' in a LABS run co-ordinated with a timely explosion and mushroom cloud from the Laffans Plain area.

Sadly, it has to be acknowledged that the Scimitar had significant limitations in the pure fighter role. At high altitude its manoeuvrability was poor, easily 'pitching up' due probably to its relatively thick wing section. Furthermore, it had no air intercept radar, nor modern navigational system, requiring the Mark I Eyeball to work overtime! Although not related to its performance in the air, a complicated fuel system provided the aircraft with incontinent habits which ensured that the 'drip' trays were usually well filled by the end of the overnight maintenance watch!

Ironically, with its first class low-speed handling qualities, a fine pilot's view over the short nose, an in-flight refuelling capability and a robust undercarriage, the Scimitar was clearly well suited for deck operations at sea. In my view the Scimitar provided an excellent transition from the Sea Hawk into the swept-wing era. For me it was a pilot's aircraft through and through, a delight to fly and remembered with affection.

Right: Lieutenant-Commander Leppard accepts airfield transport on behalf of the 807 Squadron aerobatic team from the Managing Director of Triumph Motorcycles, Farnborough, September 1959.

The SBAC show at Farnborough in 1959 saw 807 Squadron demonstrating its prowess in the air in front of the huge crowds gathered for the event.

Top: Two Scimitars, their display completed, come into land.

Above: XD248 taxies in, its air brakes still deployed and its outer wing panels just beginning to fold.

Right: The team: (left to right) Lieutenant-Commander T. C. S. Leece (SP), Lieutenant P. J. Lovick (Staff Officer), Lieutenant-Commander K. A. Leppard (CO), Lieutenant D. Pentreath, Lieutenant G. B. Hoddinott, Sub-Lieutenant I. McE. B. Aitchison and Lieutenant P. H. Perks (AWI).

Opposite: Practice makes perfect: 807 rehearse their 'Box Four' formation off the Sussex coast, September 1959.

COURTESY COLIN CASPERD

SEVENTY-NINE

SCIMITAR

SECOND-LINE SCIMITAR SQUADRONS

Unit	Dates	Commanding Officer(s)	Remarks
700X Flight	27/08/57–29/05/58	Cdr T. G. Innes AFC Lt-Cdr W. A. Tofts (acting) (21/03/58)	Intensive Flying Trials Unit (IFTU). Based at Ford.
700 Naval Air Squadron	00/03/58–00/02/59	Cdr T. G. Innes AFC ? Cdr J. D. Russell (17/04/58)	Commissioned at Ford, moved to Yeovilton September 1958. Scimitars on strength from March 1958.
736 Naval Air Squadron	00/06/59–26/03/65	Lt-Cdr J. D. Baker Lt-Cdr A. J. Mancais (02/05/60) Lt-Cdr P. G. Newman (09/10/61) Lt-Cdr J. A. D. Ford (10/01/63) Lt-Cdr J. Worth (09/12/63)	Principal Scimitar training unit. Based at Lossiemouth. First Scimitars received June 1959.
764 Naval Air Squadron	00/02/59–00/06/59	Lt-Cdr D. T. McKeown Lt-Cdr R. M. P. Carne (20/04/59)	Briefly the Scimitar training unit before role assumed by 736.
764B Flight	26/03/65–23/11/65	Lt-Cdr J. Worth Lt-Cdr D. T. McKeown (17/06/57)	Succeeded 736 as Scimitar training. requirements reduced.

OTHER UNIT

Fleet Requirements Unit			Civilian operator (Airwork Ltd). Miscellaneous Fleet tasks. Based at Hurn.

Right and below: Early-production Scimitars XD221 (right) and XD220 (below) seen engaged in proving trials on board HMS *Victorious* in September 1958. The aircraft are assigned to 700 Squadron, which took over the duties of 700X Flight when the latter disbanded in May 1958.

THE BACKSIDE OF THE DRAG CURVE

Lieutenant-Commander Colin Casperd

I joined 700X Flight at RNAS Ford in March 1958. This was the Trials and Development Flight and had been in existence for a few months, staffed by some test pilot graduates and with its numbers augmented by other fairly experienced fighter pilots. The Flight was due to form the first Scimitar squadron, 803, in June at Lossiemouth and I was one of about half a dozen appointed to make up the numbers for the Squadron. We were all day fighter pilots with at least one tour behind us; I had done a little more and was a QFI and an Instrument Examiner and so took on the role of Instrument Examiner for 803 Squadron.

The introduction to the Scimitar was rather basic, although we did attend an engines course at Rolls-Royce Derby. The nearest thing to a simulator was a big box in the corner of the hangar with a seat, pictures and some instruments. Nothing moved, apart from the 'helper' standing behind: he was the well-known 'Harpic', our electrical officer, who had probably put it together in the first place. He was known for that sort of thing.

The Flight worked very long hours, with maintenance throughout the night, and we flew most of the daylight hours. I note that my familiarisation flights were on the same day, 19 March, landing from the second at 1820—not dark, but presumably darkish—and for the next trip I was airborne at 0730. Sometimes with these early starts, and depending on our task, using our speed and range we would 'exercise' other air stations by arriving overhead at 0800 and calling up with some form of exercise emergency—good training for all concerned (and at least *we* enjoyed it!).

General memories of these days of the Scimitar were that it was a mighty beast with masses of power, was supersonic in a very gentle descent and would reach 40,000 feet in four minutes from a standing start as long as you did not try to dash off with the Palouste starter still plugged in. The overriding memory, however, was of trying to slow to the backside of the drag curve, then putting on power to keep it there when downwind in the landing circuit. I eventually achieved it, but not without one slight incident. I knew Ford from before the war (as a child) and had also been stationed there with an Attacker squadron (803 again) in 1953, and for the Attacker the runways were adequate. However, the Scimitar, much heavier and faster, liked to have a dry runway and good brakes—and, of course, the correct approach speed. Perhaps I had all those, apart from the dry runway. It was pouring with rain, and I ended up in the grass at the north-east end of the main runway. It was then a matter of pulling the aircraft backwards on to the runway, but when this was attempted it sank further into the mud, and the problem was only solved by the use of steel plates (PSP). All was then well—except that the airfield was closed for the day!

We generally flew twice or three times a day on a variety of trials, fuel consumption tests, checking temperatures in various parts of the aircraft and generally building up the flying hours in order to discover and rectify any maintenance problems. For example, firing the cannon would on occasion result in a hydraulic failure—not a happy situation with an aircraft whose flying controls were all hydraulic powered.

Most of my memories are about the Flight generally— one pilot who had a hunting horn, another who, on entering the crew room in the morning would immediately phone his bookmaker quoting his betting name 'Rocketship'. Then there were the four pilots returning from Arundel one evening in a Riley sports coupé, which failed to take a corner very well and rolled. No one was hurt enough to be off the next day's flying programme. I also recall conducting four instrument rating tests on the same day so that everybody was up to date before relocating to Lossiemouth to form 803 Squadron.

We experienced tragedy when on 20 March 1958 our CO, Tom Innes, was killed in a car crash. I had known him for years: he had been both SP and then CO of my Attacker squadron, 803. His place was taken by Des Russell, who took the Flight to Lossiemouth to form 803 Scimitar Squadron but was himself also tragically killed carrying out the first Squadron deck landing aboard *Victorious*.

Owing to an accident, I left the Squadron at this time, to return later.

Left: A gleaming, brand new Scimitar, XD230, in maintenance at RNAS Ford, spring 1958. Note the practice of painting the serial number and 'Royal Navy' legend in black at this time—a practice that would change in later years. XD224 can just be glimpsed beyond the starboard wing

Above: Practising for Farnborough, 1962: 'Fred's Five' Sea Vixens of 766 Squadron and four Scimitars of 736 Squadron in 'Box Nine', the formation led by Lieutenant-Commander P. Reynolds.

Left: The five pilots of the 736 Squadron aerobatic team: (left to right) CO Lieutenant-Commander Pete Newman (leader), Lieutenant A. H. S. ('Paddy') Anderson (No 2, port wingman), SP Lieutenant-Commander John Kennett (No 3, starboard wingman), QFI Lieutenant Pete De Souza (singleton) and AWI Lieutenant Bob Edward (No 4, box).

Right: Four gleaming 736 NAS Scimitars line up for take-off at the 1962 SBAC Display at Farnborough.

BOX NINE

Lieutenant-Commander Bob Edward

For the 1962 Farnborough display, 736 Squadron at RNAS Lossiemouth was tasked to provide a four-plane formation aerobatic team to act with a singleton, the whole to be co-ordinated with a five-plane aero team from a Sea Vixen squadron from RNAS Yeovilton. Initial practice commenced on 1 June 1962, the display having been scheduled for 3 September. Three months' training was deemed sufficient.

736 was a training squadron with a CO, SP, AWI, QFI and two unqualified instructors, one of whom was the Simulator Officer. The normal student intake was three courses each of three trainees, ranging from OFS (*ab initio* pilots) to COs-designate of the four front-line Scimitar squadrons. The training task continued until 24 July, at which stage the air station went on summer leave. Flying recommenced on 14 August with a reduced student load.

In addition to practising formation aeros and teaching students air warfare tactics and weapon delivery, two major inter-service firepower demonstrations were carried out—'Saucy Sue', an international demonstration in the English Channel, and 'Noisy Nora', a 'home' demonstration (but including foreign military attachés) on Salisbury Plain. These involved co-ordinated attacks on splash targets and smoke floats in the Channel and mock-up military targets on the Larkhill live range.

In June I flew twenty-five formation aerobatic sorties, chiefly in the evening after student day flying had been completed and before night flying commenced. (Night flying at Lossie in the summer? Yes, but it was commonly called 'NEWDs'—Night Exercises Without Darkness!) In July I flew twenty-one similar sorties and in August eighteen. These included a press display and a display at RNAS Abbotsinch, which is now Glasgow Airport.

On 20 August we moved to RNAS Yeovilton to begin full-time working-up with the Sea Vixens, and on 30 August we moved to Farnborough, where we lived in the Empire Test Pilots' Mess and were made most welcome and comfortable. On 1 September we had a final rehearsal. The SBAC event covered seven days, on the last of which, at the end of the show, we returned to Lossie. Pete Newman was interviewed by BBC Television and ended the programme by marching down the Farnborough runway into the sunset playing the bagpipes!

The RN display started in mid-afternoon with a combined loop of five Sea Vixens with four Scimitars forming a 'Box Nine'. When we were at the top of the loop the singleton roared in at 0.97 Mach and took a photograph of the VIP enclosure. On pull-out from the loop there was a co-ordinated display of rolls, twinkle rolls, tight turns and a slow pass hook-down before the Scimitars landed and the Vixens went back to Yeovilton. The RN Photo Team then developed the film and about half an hour after we landed distributed copy prints to the startled VIPs showing them with their heads back and mouths open, watching the loop!

Our routine was very relaxed. In the morning there was the admin, and then a visit to the trade caravans. Lunch was kindly given by various firms and was quite super, but one did have to limit the alcohol intake! Then we strolled over to the hangars at the north end of the runway, got the brief, started up and took off. On completion of the display we returned to the companies' caravans and could start the serious business of drinking 'Horse's Necks' made with Courvoisier brandy.

The pilots were provided with motor scooters by one particularly generous firm, which we were allowed to use from the time we arrived at Farnborough until we left—for runs ashore as well as about the base. We all had to obtain motorcycle licences, for which a certain amount of training was required. The RN provided the training on large dispatch riders' bikes at Lossie and our tests were passed (no failures) in Elgin.

The following weekend 736 did a five-aircraft display for Battle of Britain shows at RAF Acklington and RAF Leuchars, and that was the end of the 736 Squadron 1962 Formation Displays. It was a lot of work—and a lot of fun!

Above: Scimitars of 700X Squadron at RNAS Ford in March 1958; all but the sixth aircraft from the camera have the original nose profile. Note the varied styles of call-signs and fin code ('F' for Ford)'.

Left: XD231 of 736 Squadron at Lee-on-Solent in August 1962, still carrying the original style of tailfin adornment, the station code in white.

Right: 736 Squadron was essentially the Scimitar training unit and thus virtually all Scimitar trainee pilots would have passed through its OFS courses prior to appointment to a front-line squadron. The author served as the AWI in 736 for a year from September 1962.

Left: 736 NAS Scimitars at Lossiemouth in mid-1961. The aircraft nearest the camera has yet to receive its blue lightning flash on the fin. The Squadron aircraft call-signs were painted in black and white, their style distinctive amongst Scimitar units.

Right: 764 Squadron's relationship with the Scimitar was very brief, lasting only for a couple of months in early 1959, its task being taken up by 736. 764B Flight's was a little more intense, lasting through 1965 as Scimitars were transferred from 736, by now fully occupied with Buccaneer training. This photograph shows a retired 764B aircraft at RNAS Culdrose.